GUITAR *signature licks*

Deep Purple
Greatest Hits

by Troy Stetina

Cover photo by Ken Settle

ISBN 0-634-02942-8

HAL•LEONARD®
CORPORATION
7777 W. BLUEMOUND RD. P.O. BOX 13819 MILWAUKEE, WI 53213

For all works contained herein:
Unauthorized copying, arranging, adapting, recording or public performance is an infringement of copyright.
Infringers are liable under the law.

Visit Hal Leonard Online at
www.halleonard.com

CONTENTS

Section:	Page:	CD track:
Introduction	4	
About the Author	6	
The Songs	7	
The Recording	7	
Tuning	7	1
Black Night	8	2-5
Strange Kind of Woman	13	6-11
Lazy	18	12-13
Highway Star	22	14-17
Space Truckin'	32	18-21
Smoke on the Water	38	22-27
Woman From Tokyo	45	28-29
Burn	48	30-33
Knocking at Your Back Door	51	34-37
Hush	59	38-41
Guitar Notation Legend	64	

INTRODUCTION

Over the years, Deep Purple has evolved into a veritable hard rock institution, launching multiple careers from its ever-changing lineup. Once credited in the Guinness Book of World Records as the world's loudest band, the group has evolved from rock/pop cover-songs in its embryonic days to classical experimentation, heavy metal mayhem, and progressive hard rock. The one constant factor marked throughout has been a philosophy of taking things to the very limit—and breaking the rules. As guitarist Ritchie Blackmore once said, "The whole point of Deep Purple, what made it tick, was that we refused to bow down to anybody. Musically or personality-wise. We would just say, 'Fuck it.' And we meant it, and that bothered some people. But it's what gave us an edge." This edge, combined with their virtuosic musicianship and trademark improvisational forays, would come to produce some of the most powerful, evocative, and momentous rock music ever recorded. Deep Purple has undoubtedly earned a unique place in music history and influenced a generation.

The Beginning

The story of the band begins in Hertford, England, in February 1968. Chris Curtis, former drummer for the Searchers (a band whose popularity once rivaled the Beatles in early-1960s Britain), sensed change was afoot amid the psychedelic explosion of the Beatles' *Sgt. Pepper's* album and the emerging harder-edged bands such as Cream, the Jeff Beck Group, and The Jimi Hendrix Experience. He formed a loose-knit new group—which he dubbed "Roundabout"—with classically trained keyboardist Jon Lord and an exceptional young guitarist named Ritchie Blackmore. Although Curtis would exit quickly, the dual talents of Lord and Blackmore would come to define much of the evolving sound that would become Deep Purple.

Guitarist Richard Hugh Blackmore was born April 14, 1945 in Weston, England. At the age of 10, his father had bought him a guitar and paid for classical lessons. While still in school, Blackmore picked up the electric guitar and excelled by all accounts. Coincidentally, he also happened to live on the same street as "Big Jim" Sullivan (guitarist for Tom Jones). As the story goes, a young Ritchie often came knocking with guitar in hand. "[Sullivan] was just about the best guitarist in England," says Blackmore, "He taught me a lot of tricks." By age 17, Ritchie was cutting records and thereafter began to hone his trademark, stony "Man in Black" image while touring with The Outlaws—backing up stars such as Jerry Lee Lewis and, in the process, developing a reputation for rampant destruction. (Blackmore says they were rarely asked back after gigs!) When the invitation to join Roundabout was extended to him, he was living in Hamburg, Germany. Tired of playing other artists' music, he was ready for a change and a more forward-leaning sound.

Roundabout, however, proved "looser" than anyone had imagined—the group's creator promptly left a month after founding it! Bassist Nick Semper and keyboardist Jon Lord then recruited vocalist Rod Evans to replace him, and drummer Ian Paice came along as well. Together with Blackmore, they embarked on a brief tour of Denmark, playing their first gig on April 20, 1968. The band soon felt their name didn't benefit them. Blackmore suggested "Deep Purple," and although it wasn't agreed to immediately, it stuck. Deep Purple Mark I (as this lineup would eventually be labeled by fans) released three albums. These chronicled the new band's search to define itself. The first, *Shades of Deep Purple* (July, 1968), was mostly cover songs. One of those covers, "Hush," was released as a single. Ignored in the U.K., it scored a surprise Top 5 hit in the U.S. Their second album, *The Book of Taliesyn* (October, 1968), slipped in more original material—including some classical stylings in the form of synthesized strings. The third album, simply titled *Deep Purple* (1969), was the harbinger of things to come—the first that really hinted toward the heavier direction that would follow.

As their live shows grew louder and even downright explosive, they were steadily distancing themselves from their rock/pop origins. Blackmore toyed with extended feedback noise, or "chance music" as he has called it, and songs were routinely extended into lengthy showcases to display the members' considerable individual talents. Inspired by the success of heavy-rock contemporaries Led Zeppelin and Black Sabbath, they decided to be even bolder and more experimental. To do so, however, they needed to make some changes. At this point, vocalist Ian Gillan and bassist Roger Glover replaced Rod Evans and Nick Simper.

Deep Purple's Golden Era

Deep Purple Mark II is the lineup most of us recognize as the "classic" Deep Purple: Ian Gillan, Ritchie Blackmore, Roger Glover, Ian Paice, and John Lord. Curiously, however, their first album together was actually *Concerto For Group and Orchestra*, recorded live with the Royal Philharmonic Orchestra on September 24, 1969. It was the follow-up release, *Deep Purple in Rock* (1970), that moved the band clearly into the hard rock arena where they finally found their unified, collective voice. This album was an unqualified success in both the U.S. and Europe, hailing the arrival of the band's most prolific period. *Fireball* (1971) quickly followed to even greater success. Then, *Machine Head* (1972) vaulted the band to superstardom, selling two million copies in the U.S. in a single year.

By this time, the relentless pressure and constant touring was beginning to show in the form of personality clashes. Still, the band managed to hold on for perhaps their most powerful live performances ever, which were recorded (in 1972) and released in the double-live album, *Made in Japan*. Deep Purple Mark II also managed yet one more studio album as well, *Who Do We Think We Are*, in 1973.

Shortly after the release, while the album was riding high on the charts, Ian Gillan and Roger Glover announced their retirements from the band. The remaining three members of Deep Purple forged ahead, recruiting vocalist David Coverdale and bassist/vocalist Glenn Hughes.

"Revolving Door"

The new DP Mk III released *Burn* in February 1974, with the tandem vocal efforts of Coverdale and Hughes pulling the band's style in a distinctly bluesy direction. It was a powerful comeback. *Stormbringer* followed in November 1974, but to lesser success. In fact, Blackmore was already becoming disenchanted with the band's gradual shift toward the funkier "white soul sound" and had already begun to save his best songs for his planned solo album. He left in April, 1975 to form Rainbow. To the surprise of many, Deep Purple continued and the seemingly irreplaceable guitarist was replaced—by American-born guitarist Tommy Bolin.

The DP Mk IV lineup released just one album, *Come Taste the Band* (1975), and toured until March 1976. After things fell apart, Bolin went back to record his second solo album. But tragedy followed Tommy; he died of a drug overdose in Miami on December 4, 1976, while on tour in support of Jeff Beck.

At this point, it seemed that the Deep Purple saga was history. Everyone went their separate ways—some criss-crossing, and some not. Jon Lord formed Paice, Ashton & Lord. Glen Hughes went with Trapeze. David Coverdale formed Whitesnake in 1978, brought Jon Lord on board later that year, and added Ian Paice the next. Meanwhile, Ian Gillan, who had left Deep Purple in 1973, had gone on to form the Ian Gillan band and enjoyed considerable success everywhere except the U.S. (but for his solo performance in the soundtrack of *Jesus Christ Superstar*). In 1983, Gillan was touring with Black Sabbath, where, oddly enough, he replaced former Rainbow vocalist Ronnie James Dio.

Roger Glover had also kept busy—as a producer, working with bands like Judas Priest and Nazareth, as well as Gillan, Rainbow, and Whitesnake, and as a bassist, joining Rainbow in 1978.

Reunion

So it was with some surprise that the news of a Deep Purple reunion was greeted. The Mark II lineup, which had spawned their biggest successes, was back together again! And after 10 years, the energetic quintet of Gillan, Blackmore, Glover, Paice, and Lord was as strong and creatively vital as ever with *Perfect Strangers* (1984). Explains Glover, "Purple is like an old love affair... And love can be very close to hate. Friction was the thing that caused this band to split in 1973, but friction was also the thing that gave us the success we enjoyed in 1973." But how long could the group remain united before personal tensions once again rent them apart? By the follow-up 1987 release *The House of Blue Light*, the old issues had resurfaced. It was over in the summer of 1988, after the live *Nobody's Perfect*, when Ian left for the second time.

1990 to Present

Deep Purple then shocked fans again by continuing with a replacement for Gillan. American vocalist Joe Lynn Turner, who had worked with Blackmore for a time in Rainbow (as well as with Blackmore-admirer Yngwie Malmsteen) joined the group in 1990, giving us DP Mk VI. But the fans weren't buying it. Gillan stayed close enough to return—again—in 1992, forming Mk VII. Before long, Ian and Ritchie were at each other's throats, but this time it was Blackmore who called it quits.

Joe Satriani stepped in for a long live tour beginning in December 1993 (Mk VIII). Word has it that the band rehearsed once before their first live show in Japan, which went off without a hitch. Due to contractual obligations, Satriani left in 1994 and was replaced by former Dixie Dregs guitarist and virtuoso in his own right, Steve Morse. Deep Purple Mk IX released *Perpendicular* in 1995 and embarked on a world tour shortly afterward in support. At the time of this writing, Mk IX was the current lineup.

But the question buried deep has to remain, "Is there a possible second Mk II reunion yet ahead?" Who can say? After all, the legendary lineup splintered in the early 1970s, then came back as strong as ever a decade later, only to split apart once again a few short years later. And as they say, sometimes history repeats itself.

ABOUT THE AUTHOR

Troy Stetina is a world-renowned guitarist and leading music educator. He has written more than 30 books and methods for Hal Leonard Corporation including *Speed Mechanics for Lead Guitar, Metal Rhythm Guitar Vol. 1 and 2*, and *Metal Lead Guitar Vol. 1 and 2*, as well as Signature Licks books *Best of Black Sabbath, Best of Rage Against the Machine, Best of Foo Fighters, Aggro-Metal,* and *Best of Ozzy Osbourne.* Troy's latest CD is *Exottica.* Visit him on the web at *www.stetina.com* for free lessons and tips!

THE SONGS

The songs appearing in this book are the following:

"Black Night"—from *Deepest Purple: The Very Best of Deep Purple*, 1980
(Originally released as a single by Warner Brothers, 1970)
"Strange Kind of Woman"—from *Deepest Purple: The Very Best of Deep Purple*, 1980
(Originally released on *Fireball*, 1971)
"Lazy"—from *Nobody's Perfect*, 1988
(Originally released on *Made in Japan*, 1973)
"Highway Star"—from *Deepest Purple: The Very Best of Deep Purple*, 1980
(Originally released on *Machine Head*, 1972)
"Space Truckin'"—from *Deepest Purple: The Very Best of Deep Purple*, 1980
(Originally released on *Machine Head*, 1972)
"Smoke on the Water"—from *Deepest Purple: The Very Best of Deep Purple*, 1980
(Originally released on *Machine Head*, 1972)
"Woman from Tokyo"—from *Deepest Purple: The Very Best of Deep Purple*, 1980
(Originally released on *Who Do We Think We Are*, 1973)
"Burn"—from *Deepest Purple: The Very Best of Deep Purple*, 1980
(Originally released on *Burn*, 1974)
"Knocking at Your Back Door"—from *Perfect Strangers*, 1984
"Hush"—from *Nobody's Perfect*, 1988

THE RECORDING

The accompanying audio CD includes note-for-note performances of the indicated song excerpts. Great care has been taken to recreate the tones of the original recordings except in regard to the stereo spread—the featured guitar part is isolated in the right channel, while the backing band and other supporting guitar parts are isolated in the left channel. Therefore, by using your stereo's balance control, you may hear the entire band, or isolate the guitar part for learning purposes, or play along with the backing tracks. And of course, you may fine-tune the balance control to create any relative blend of instruments that you wish.

    Guitars and bass: Troy Stetina
    Organ/keys: Dave Hoefler
    Drums: Scott Schroedl

Recorded, mixed, and mastered at Artist Underground, New Berlin, Wisconsin.
Produced by Troy Stetina.

TUNING

All the songs on this CD are played in standard tuning:

 Standard tuning (low to high): E–A–D–G–B–E

BLACK NIGHT
Words and Music by Ritchie Blackmore, Roger Glover, Jon Lord and Ian Paice

Figure 1–Intro, Verse, and Chorus

"Black Night" harkens back to the early days of the band's prolific second lineup (Mark II), featuring Gillan, Blackmore, Glover, Paice, and Lord. It was tracked during the studio sessions for *Deep Purple in Rock* in October, 1969 and February, 1970 at the IBC, De Lane Lea, and Abbey Road studios in London, and displays the new heavier rock direction toward which the group was heading. This cut, however, was actually left off the album at the time. When later released as a single in May 1970, it scored the band's first big hit in the U.K., rising to #2 on the charts. It also quickly became regarded as a classic by fans, and later appeared on *Deepest Purple: The Very Best of Deep Purple* (1980). And a remixed, unedited (and significantly longer) version appeared on the anniversary re-issue of *Deep Purple in Rock* (1995). Several live performances of the tune populate other albums as well.

Based in the key of E minor, the riff draws upon each note of E minor pentatonic (E–G–A–B–D) in the context of an uptempo, bluesy shuffle. Though written as eighth notes, notice the shuffle rhythm indication at the beginning of the transcription. This says that eighth notes are to be played as a triplet figure consisting of the first note lasting two-thirds of the beat and the last note lasting one-third of the beat. Listen to the audio to hear the rhythmic effect of this.

At the verse, the guitar drops back to support the vocals, with a D–E (♭7–root) move followed by low-octave, open E mutes. Use the palm, or heel, of your picking hand to lightly cover and muffle the ends of the strings at the bridge saddles.

After six measures of verse, we see a surprise move to a single-note melody line focusing on E–D–F♯–E (root–♭7–2–root) with E minor pentatonic connecting tones. This finishes off the eight-measure verse with a quarter-note triplet that walks down to A.

The progression here is a repeated A5–G5–E5 progression, which Blackmore decorates expressively. Over A5, he favors an A minor pentatonic approach, beginning with a quick trill (G–A). Over G5, it is sparser, suggesting a G7 arpeggio with the prominent F (♭7) tone. Then, he rips a pentatonic lick over the two measures of E5, replete with stinging vibrato-bar shakes. The lick utilizes the common E minor pentatonic "box 1" shape at the twelfth fret. Temporary pauses on E, G, and octave E/B dyad give the lick a rhythmic quality that seems to stress the downbeat of 2, followed by the upbeat of 3, then the upbeat 3 again in the next measure.

Measure 21 begins with the same A5–G5 move, but ends on B5 (the V chord), creating a "half close." That is, it exerts a harmonic tension, which pulls to resolve to the tonic at the beginning of the next section—in this case, the riff. This transition effect is further emphasized by the rhythmic break at this point.

Notice that the chorus lyric, "Black night," enters here (measure 21) on the second A5. The improvisationally oriented Blackmore also embellishes this second A5–G5 in a slightly different way. Though still focusing strongly on minor 7ths, he chooses a modified set of passing tones at beat 4 of each chord, pulling to the target pitches of 5ths from a half step below in each case.

© 1970 (Renewed 1998) B. FELDMAN & CO. LTD. trading as HEC MUSIC
All Rights for the United States and Canada Controlled and Administered by GLENWOOD MUSIC CORP.
All Rights Reserved   International Copyright Secured   Used by Permission

Figure 2–Guitar Solo

The solo occurs over an extended verse pattern. Anchored firmly in E minor, Ritchie relies heavily on wild whammy-bar tricks, one trademark element of his distinct soloing style. Tonal variety is also achieved through the alternating use of E minor pentatonic and diatonic approaches.

Measure 1 opens in E minor pentatonic with a quick blues-inspired, staccato slide up to B (5th), followed by a lengthy G (♭3rd) sustained amid wide bar-induced vibrato. An oblique dyad bend follows in measure 3, with similar treatment. Measure 4 then completes the first phrase with a half step bend-release-bend-release move that toys between the diatonic 2nd step and minor 3rd.

After a pickup-note slide and high C, measure 5 opens with a full-step bend up to the melodically dissonant B♭ (♭5th). Coming down, we see the unusual set of tones, C–B♭–A–G, then G–G♯–G–E, suggesting a temporary E Locrian modality followed by an E minor pentatonic move with an added major 3rd (G♯). Never one prone to obeying the "rules," Blackmore can easily be imagined selecting tones and creating his own scales "on the fly" in an improvisational flurry!

The downward-spiraling lick continues in the E pentatonic/blues scale, first in the "box 2" area (or "upper extension"), then shifting down into twelfth-position "box 1" again. The end of measure 6 and beginning of 7 favor A, the 4th, temporarily shifting attention away from the tonic note, E. The second four-measure phrase then ends with a natural harmonic made rhythmic by use of the vibrato bar.

Things get a little crazy starting in beat 4 of measure 8. This one-beat pickup, anticipating the next phrase, which enters on beat 1 of measure 9, is produced by shaking the bar widely and quickly while at the same time fretting hammers and pulls in triplet rhythm. After two beats, the shaking gives way to simple dips of the bar on downbeats 2 and 3 of measure 9.

The remainder of measures 9–12 comes back to earth with a basically E minor pentatonic approach. Notice a few tonal discrepancies however, with a quick F natural (instead of E) in measure 10, and F♯ (instead of G) in measure 12. These brief alterations add a bit of tonal interest without changing the overall E minor pentatonic quality of the passage.

4 Featured Guitar:
Gtr. 1   meas. 1-15

5 Slow Demo:
Gtr. 1   meas. 1-12

Fig. 2

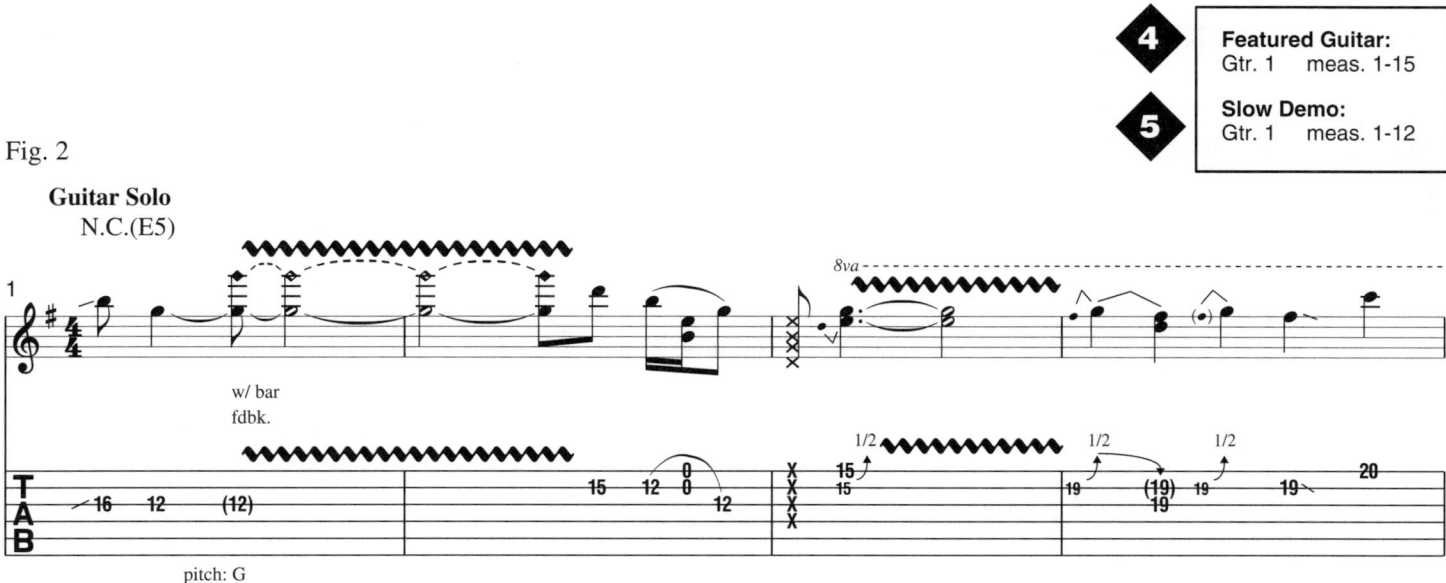

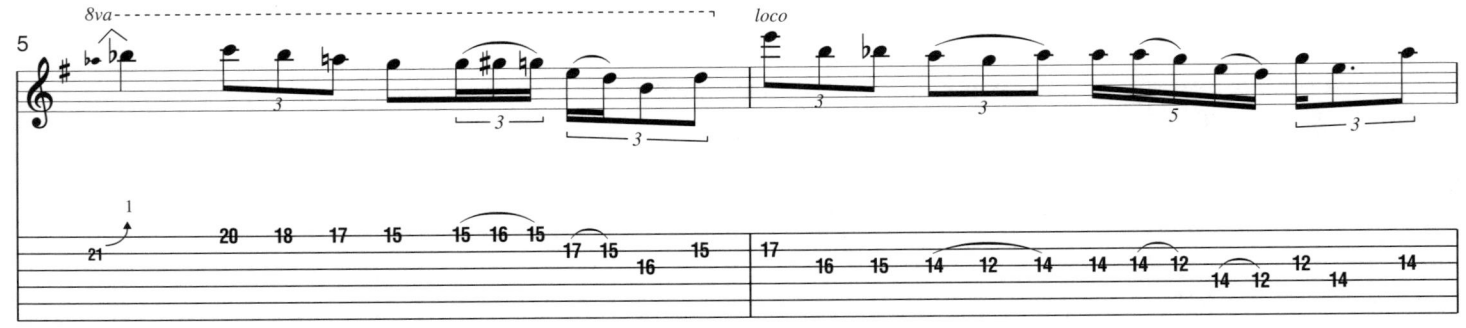
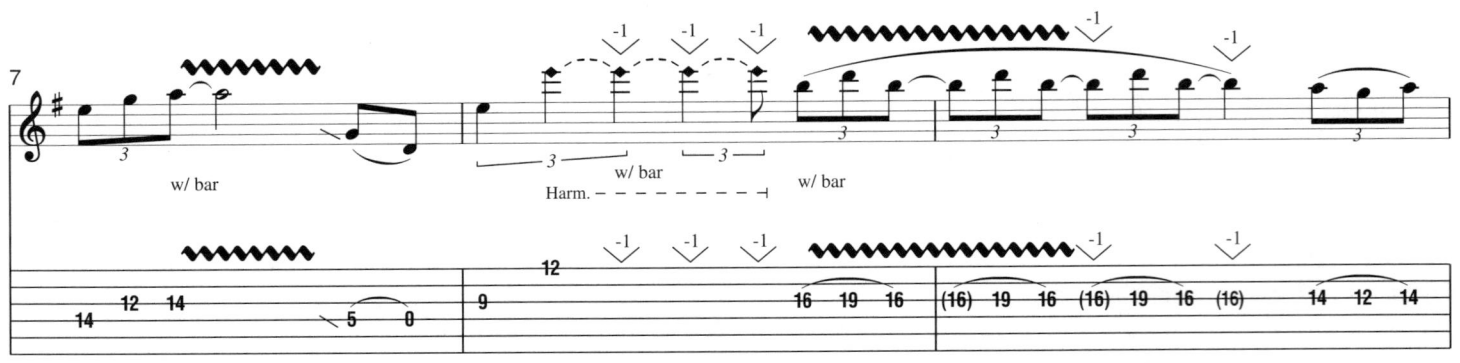
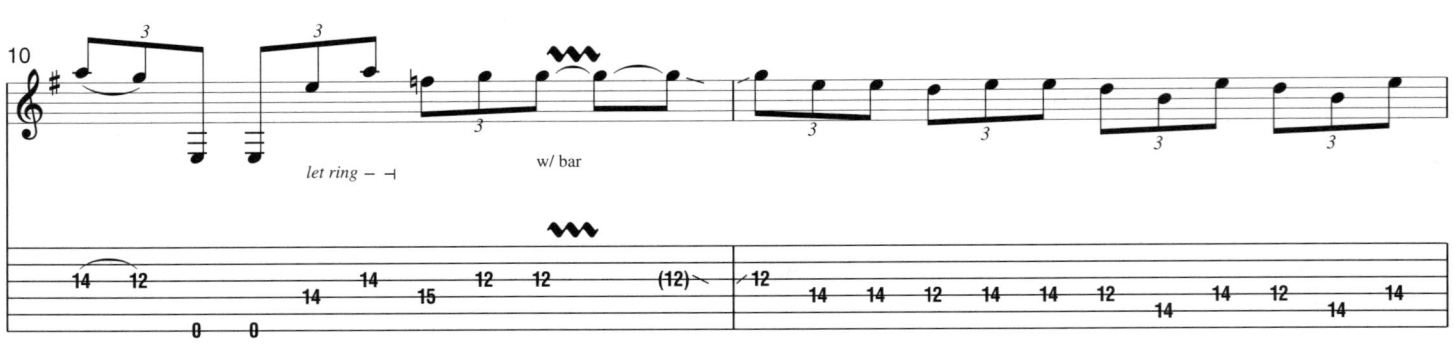

STRANGE KIND OF WOMAN

Words and Music by Ritchie Blackmore, Ian Gillan, Roger Glover, Jon Lord and Ian Paice

Figure 3–Intro, Verse, and Chorus

"Strange Kind of Woman" was recorded in 1971 in London and released on the U.S. and Japanese versions of *Fireball*. One can't help but see a strong lyrical connection between this and the later hit "Knockin' at Your Back Door." Musically, it opens with a blues-heavy passage, the treatment of which recalls Hendrix prominently. A quick staccato bend from b3rd to 4th leaps off from downbeat 1, after which the line cascades down the blues scale in the key of B minor. A single appearance of G# (6th) colors the line slightly brighter, indicating a temporary blues/Dorian mode hybrid scale. For notes appearing on adjacent strings at the same fret, try to roll pressure from one string to the next in order that they don't ring together excessively. Also, select the middle pickup throughout to re-create the slightly "boxy" tone.

In measures 3–4, the F# (V) chord applies harmonic tension. Rendered as a 7#9, or *augmented ninth*, this is the "Purple Haze chord" made famous by Hendrix.

The verse kicks in at measure 5, over a B minor pentatonic power-chord riff. Consisting of 4th dyad power chords (with low root note omitted), it spells out a B5–D5–B5–A5 then B5–D5–B5 sequence, which essentially adds up to a Bm7, harmonically speaking. Measure 7 shifts to A5-Em7, and back to the Bm7 4th dyad riff. Taken together in its barest essence, the four-measure phrase suggests the progression Bm–Bm–A–Em–Bm, or i–i–bVII–iv–i (with the A–Em filling just one measure).

What we really have here is a "riff/progression"—something in between a riff and a chord progression, with elements of both. Or, to say it another way, it's a riff that implies some overall harmonic movement. Measures 9–12 repeat the four-measure phrase.

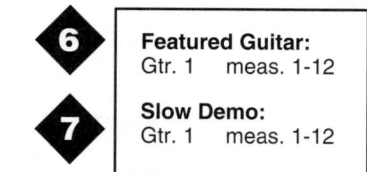

Fig. 3

© 1971 (Renewed 1999) B. FELDMAN & CO. LTD. trading as HEC MUSIC
All Rights for the United States and Canada Controlled and Administered by GLENWOOD MUSIC CORP.
All Rights Reserved   International Copyright Secured   Used by Permission

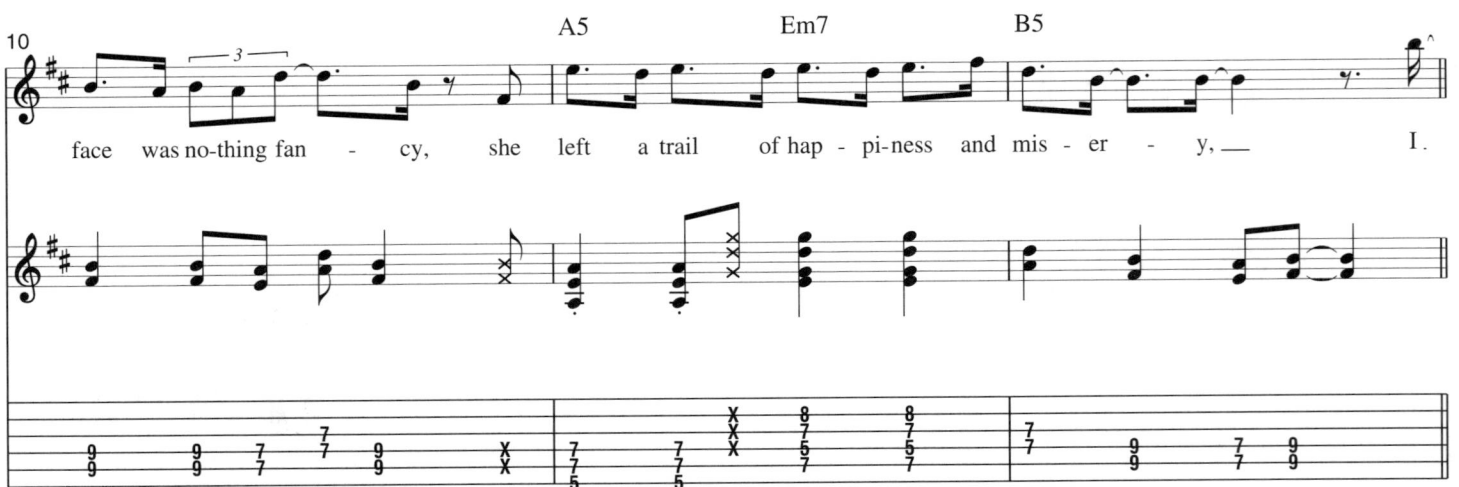

Figure 4–Chorus

The band pares it down to the basics at the chorus. Rather than a build-up of the dynamics, as is common in choruses, here we see a reduction instead, beckoning the listener to pay closer attention. (As the saying goes, "If you want to get someone's attention, whisper.") Musically, this is accomplished by the whole band playing single notes in unison, including the vocals. The result is a pinpoint narrowness of focus. The tonality is B minor pentatonic.

Notice that the harmonic movement (or progression) you see here in the chorus is exactly the same as identified within the verse riff, back in Figure 3. Good composition always manages to keep a thread of continuity running throughout, even as a song moves through changes and dynamic levels. In this case, we can see that it has been accomplished harmonically.

Figure 5–Guitar Solo

Where the solo in "Black Night" showed Ritchie Blackmore's wild, high-pitched improvisational madness, the solo of "Strange Kind of Woman" displays his other side—carefully composed and melodic. Juxtaposing these two opposing approaches is a significant element of the guitarist's style, and lends a good deal of contrast to his work.

Here, a rhythmic motif is established in measure 1 and then developed over the next three measures into a full, self-contained phrase. The scale is B minor pentatonic, in seventh position "box 1," with a temporary excursion to B natural minor by picking up C♯ (2nd) in measure 3. The entire four-measure phrase is further developed on repetition in measures 5-8.

This is a great example with which to examine Blackmore's phrasing in more detail. First, notice his penchant for leading into each phrase with pickup notes: A single A (♭7th) leads into measure 1 and measure 5. A full triplet ushers in measure 9. Later in the solo, he takes this idea one step further, revealing another signature element of his lead style. While the music usually tends to fall into four-measure phrases—and most rock guitarists would phrase their licks accordingly—Ritchie chooses instead to obscure the natural phrase boundaries. Pickup notes are one method of accomplishing this, as they slightly displace the lead phrase against its underlying rhythmic phrase. But at the start of measure 13, he employs another method—tying the end of one phrase right over and into the next. This has the effect of making the solo sound ongoing in a distinctly looser, or freer, sense.

In terms of melodic curves, this solo is also well conceived. It begins in the middle register for the first phrase (measures 1–4). Then it rises slightly in the second phrase, yet returns to familiar ground by phrase-end (measures 5–8). The third time around we start and end at the higher octave, pushing the tension a bit (measures 9–12). The fourth and final portion hits that register twice, then climbs above it to climax on a high F♯ (measures 13–16).

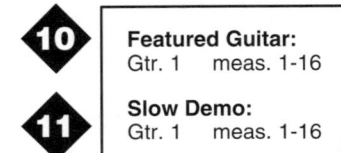

Featured Guitar:
Gtr. 1   meas. 1-16

Slow Demo:
Gtr. 1   meas. 1-16

Fig. 5

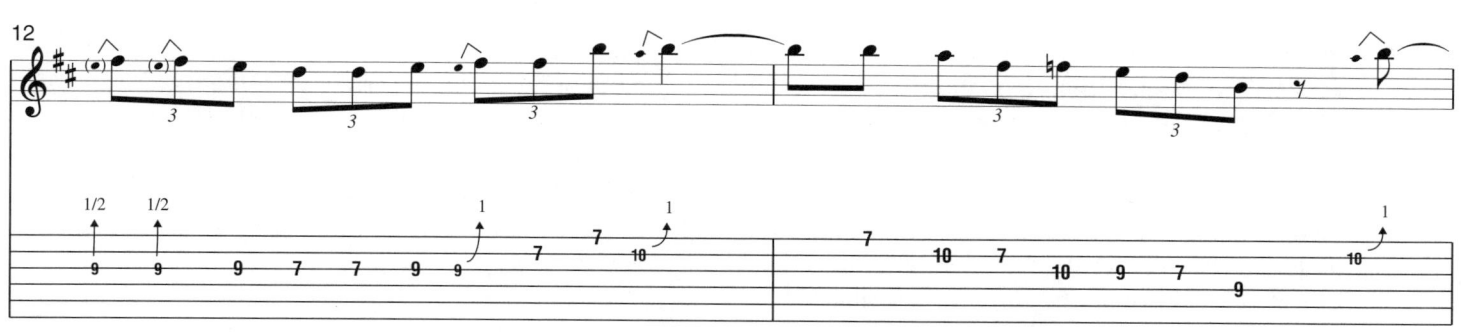

17

LAZY

Words and Music by Ritchie Blackmore, Ian Gillan, Roger Glover, Jon Lord and Ian Paice

Figure 6–Theme, Guitar Solo, Theme

"Lazy" has always been a live show highlight and first appeared on *Made in Japan* (1973). A later live version of the blues-jam showcase tune was released on *Nobody's Perfect* (1988). This transcription is of the latter version.

We pick it up at 1:26 (E), where things heat up in double time. This is played as a double-time shuffle, meaning that each pair of sixteenths is to be played in a triplet-based rhythm rather than straight (as it is written). Simply listen to the audio example as you follow the notation, and you'll catch right on.

The key is F minor. Measures 1–2 first establish a theme on Cm (the v chord). At measure 2, it begins to fall chromatically from C to B to B♭. Then the quick B♭–B–C–E♭ grouping sets up the move to Fm, the tonic chord. In measures 3–4, we see the riff repeat, now centered upon Fm. Also, notice the 3/4 measure: One beat has simply been "lopped off," allowing the next phrase to enter one beat early. This creates a sense of rhythmic interest and variety, as it always seems to sound somewhat unexpected.

Measure 5 continues on Fm. The open strings on beat 1 are essentially non-chord noise that creates a little extra harmonic "grit." With the bass and keys solidly on F, however, it still conveys an F tonal center. The remainder of measures 5–6 works from the F blues scale (F–A♭–B♭–B–C–E♭). Measures 7–8 return to Cm, to repeat the first riff motif. Notice the slight alterations here, though.

Section F (measure 9) begins the guitar solo, although the guitar itself at this point seems to be closing the previous phrase by "relaxing" on an F note for a bit. First, let's consider what the rhythm section is doing under the solo so we can view the notes in their proper context. This part is really an altered 12-bar blues progression, played twice in double time (which shortens the length to six bars). Fm is the i chord and B♭ is the IV chord. Then we see a chord substitution—where the 12-bar progression typically goes to V–IV–i–V in its closing phrase, here we see ♭III–♭VII–i–V. The ♭III and ♭VII major chords temporarily establish a strong Aeolian cadence.

Now let's look at the solo itself. Measure 9 hangs out for a little extra breathing space. Then in measure 10 we have a little F blues-scale action with the notes E♭–B–C–A♭ (♭7th–♭5th–5th–♭3rd), followed by a series of pull-offs to open G. The notes B♭–A♭–G fall into F natural minor as a 4th–♭3rd–2nd, once again showing Blackmore's penchant for mixing pentatonic with diatonic.

Over the IV chord in measure 11, he sets up a sequence pattern still utilizing the diatonic tones of F natural minor. Rhythmically, this is quite complex. Here's the trick: Listen for the rhythmic syncopation pattern created by the highest note of each grouping. This is shown above the staff in parenthesis. After you memorize the note sequences and their patterns, this is the rhythm you should feel. In other words, hit those "main" standout notes at the right time and "cram" the rest of the others in between. Not easy to do! But then, of course, this is Ritchie Blackmore. What did you expect?!

Measures 12 rises up the F natural minor scale in triplets. Measure 13 descends with added chromatic passing tones. Measure 14 goes pentatonic to close the first progression.

The second time around begins at measure 15, first in the "box 4" F minor pentatonic position, then shifting up into the "box 5" area and coming down in a quick sixteenth-triplet run. Then things get hairy in measure 16. Here you simply want to learn the patterns well, to the point where you can "cram" in the notes and come out "on your feet" at the end of the phrase by feel. Think fretboard shape, not rhythmic groupings (they are more an accidental byproduct of the "cramming" technique).

The remainder of measures 17–18 climb up the third string, drawing upon F natural minor. Blackmore remains diatonic, playing scale tones of F natural minor in measure 19 as well. Notice the "wrap-around" approach in the last three notes of measure 19, leading (and resolving) to the target note A♭ (♭3rd) at the beginning of measure 20. Blackmore often utilizes approach tones and target notes like this. Measure 20 itself re-injects F minor pentatonic after its extended hiatus, overshadowed—as it was—by F natural minor.

At Section G (measure 21) we return to the theme idea, but this time we cut past the Cm (v chord) portion and get right to the tonic-based riff. This is basically a high-register repetition of measures 3–8.

Featured Guitar:
Gtr. 1   meas. 1-26

Slow Demo:
Gtr. 1   meas. 1-26

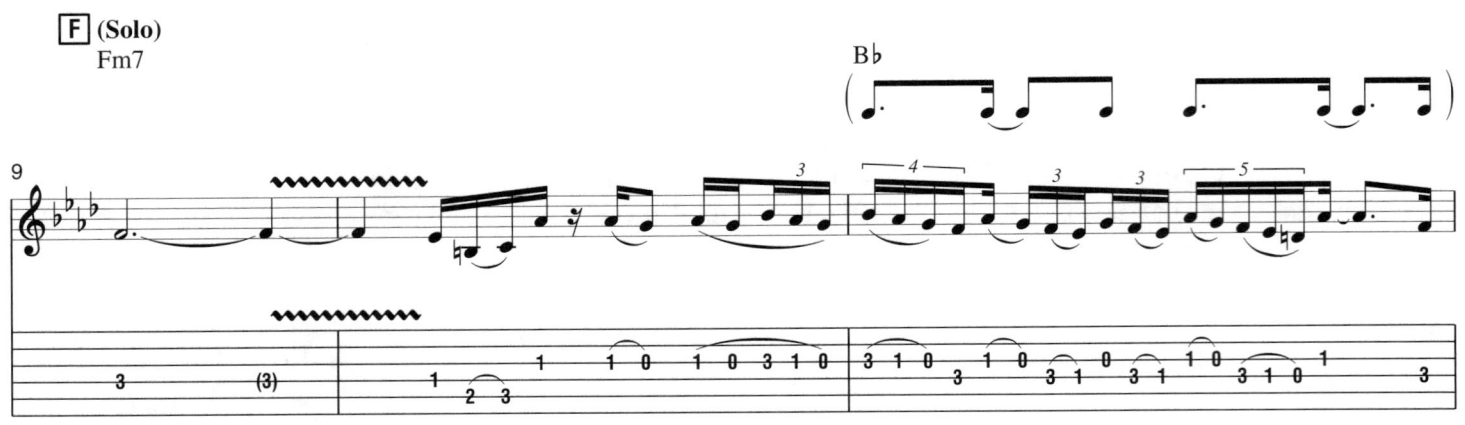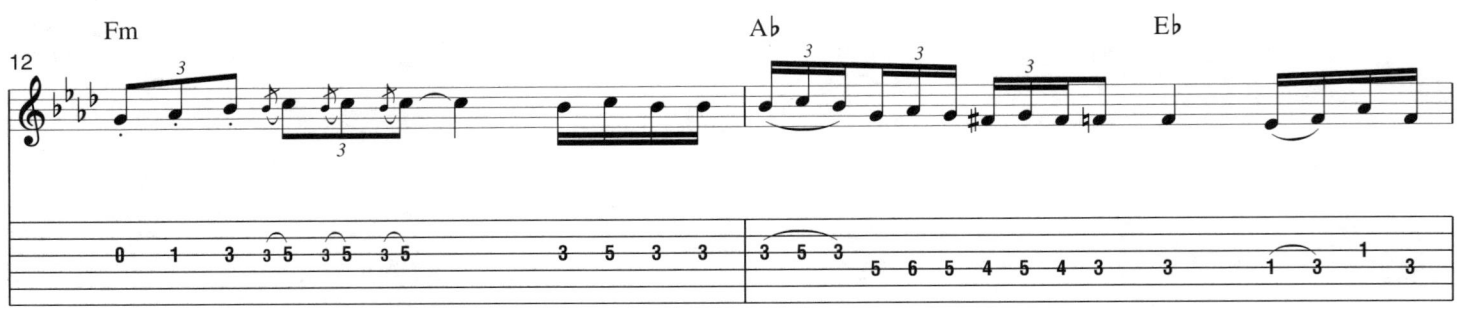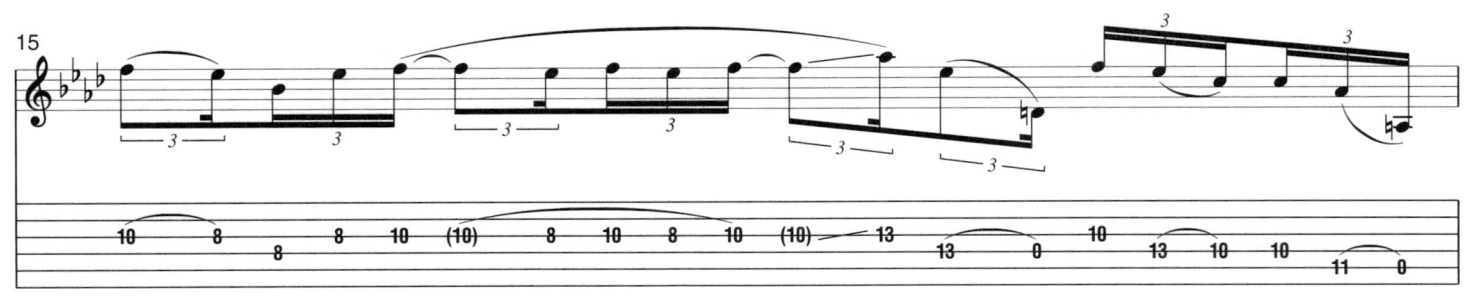

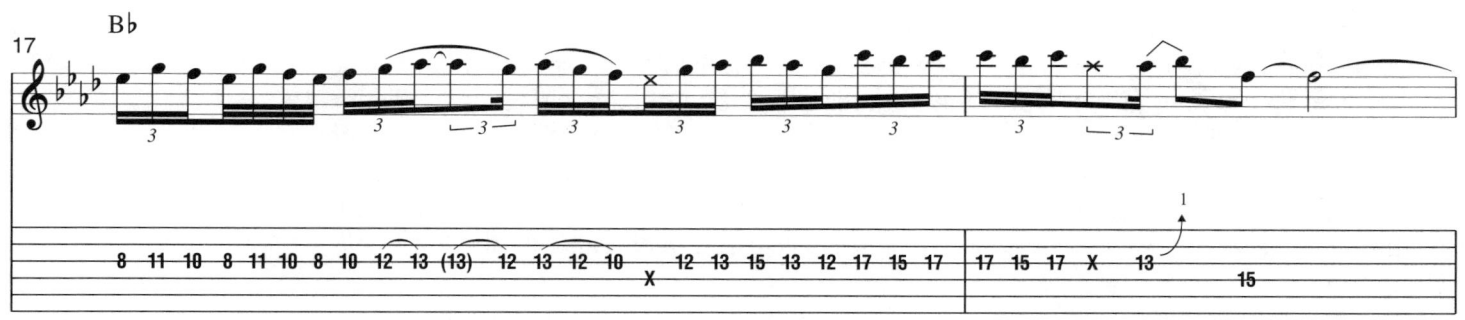
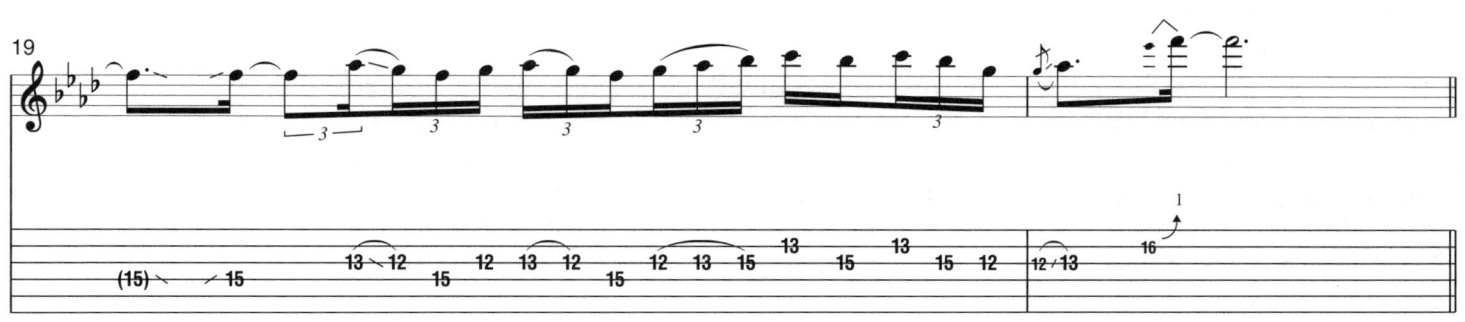
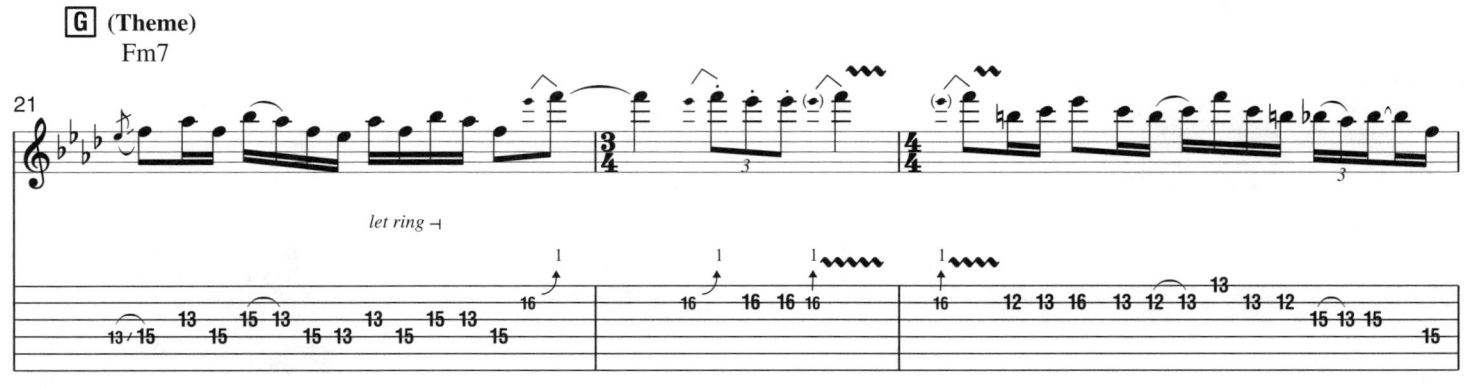

HIGHWAY STAR

Words and Music by Ritchie Blackmore, Ian Gillan, Roger Glover, Jon Lord and Ian Paice

Figure 7–Intro, Verse, Pre-Chorus, Chorus

"Highway Star" is one of the Deep Purple classics that has stood the test of time. The opening cut from their quintessential release *Machine Head* (1972), this tune helped push the album's sales past the two million mark and make Deep Purple a heavy metal household name.

The intro utilizes a series of chords incorporating a G pedal tone throughout to firmly anchor the tonal center. The G5 power chords in particular require an unusual fingering. Use your thumb to reach over the top of the neck and fret the low G, and to lightly touch and hold the fifth string mute. Your *fourth* finger should then take the octave G on the fifth fret, string 4. (The reason to use your fourth finger rather than your third will soon become apparent.) Make sure to arch it well, pressing just on the fingertip so that the open G string may also ring in unison with it. Then add D with your first finger, on the third fret, string 2.

To switch to the Fsus2/G chord, slide your first and fourth fingers down two frets, while you simultaneously replace your thumb with your third finger, to hold the fretted low G note. The next chord, C/G, is found by simply lifting your fourth finger and placing your second finger upon E, at the second fret, string 4. Now, the rationale behind the fingering becomes apparent.

Uptempo, straight-ahead palm muting drives measures 9–19, now on a standard G5 power chord. Use all downstrokes of the pick. The verse at measure 21 continues on this basic motif, now cut neatly into four-measure phrases with the B♭–C–B♭ chord moves. Overall, the verse outlines a Gm–Gm–F–D progression with various embellishments.

The pre-chorus shifts into "high gear" as the music modulates up a whole step to Am. (Relative to the original tonal center, this could also be seen as an extended ii chord.) The chorus then rises through the chords C–D–C–D, C–D–F–G, and then comes to rest on A5, the temporary new tonal center. Through this, the guitar favors single notes, playing the root of each chord.

14 Featured Guitar:
Gtr. 1   meas. 1-50

15 Slow Demos:
Gtr. 1   meas. 1-8;
21-24; 29-47

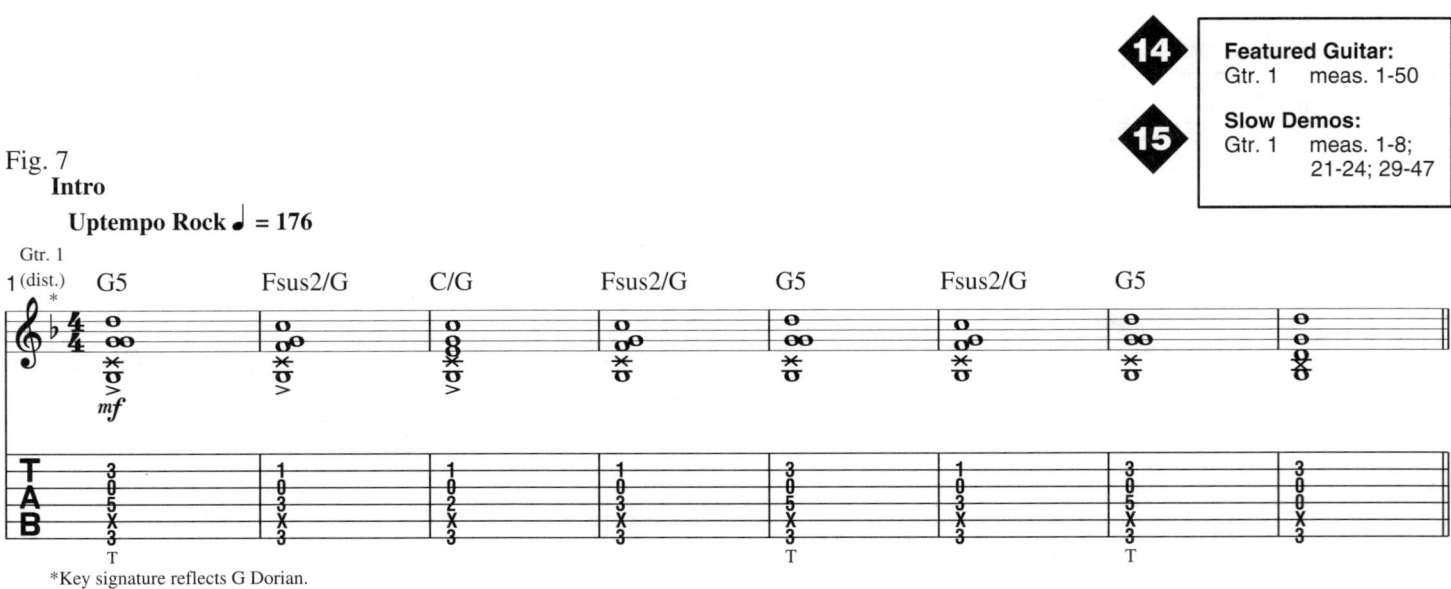

Fig. 7
Intro
Uptempo Rock ♩ = 176

*Key signature reflects G Dorian.

© 1972 (Renewed 2000) B. FELDMAN & CO. LTD. trading as HEC MUSIC
All Rights for the United States and Canada Controlled and Administered by GLENWOOD MUSIC CORP.
All Rights Reserved   International Copyright Secured   Used by Permission

Figure 8–Guitar Solo

This carefully composed and beautifully harmonized 58-measure solo is clearly one of Ritchie Blackmore's shining moments. Rarely did he in fact work out solos in advance like this, generally preferring to let things happen "in the moment." However, in this case, as he explained, "I fancied putting a bit of Mozart over that chord progression, which itself is taken from Mozart."

The harmonic underpinnings for the first sixteen bars are eight measures on D and eight measures on A. Over this, the lead favors notes of D minor pentatonic (D–F–G–A–C) and A minor pentatonic (A–C–D–E–G), respectively.

The featured guitar opens with pickup notes outlining D minor: D, F, and then a full-step bend up to octave D (or root, minor 3rd, root). Leading into measure 2, we see a similar idea, but with a strong F (♭3rd) added afterward. This is further developed in measures 3–4, as the bend becomes E up to F (2nd up to ♭3rd)—inserting a brief diatonic quality—then coming down D minor pentatonic to wrap up the first four-measure phrase. All this takes place in D minor pentatonic box 1, in tenth position. The next four measures repeat that basic idea.

Over A, we shift down to the box 1 minor pentatonic shape in fifth position. The featured part opens with repeated bends from G (♭7th) up to A (root), as the harmony guitar first reinforces in unison, then splits off to rise up to the minor 3rd. The descending lick in measures 11–12 adds an F♯ (major 6th) tone, then pushes C (minor 3rd) up to C♯ (major 3rd), brightening the line significantly as it borrows temporarily from the parallel major. Measures 13–14 continue with that concept as each C is similarly pushed upward.

The solo enters its next phase at measure 17. Here the pace seems to quicken a bit as the chords now go by every two measures. The progression is D–G–C–A. This creates a classical feel, as it is based upon a cycle of fifths cadence. That is, D is the V chord of G, and so, falls naturally to it. Then G itself is likewise the V chord of C. The shift from C down to A is the lone exception, dropping a minor 3rd. But as the phrase closes upon A, we feel the unmistakable tension of the classical "half close"—A is also the V chord and it wants to fall back to D, to begin the cycle anew.

The featured lead guitar arpeggiates the chords (D–G–C–A) in tandem with the underlying progression, further emphasizing its classical qualities. Well, they're not exactly arpeggios in the strictest sense, but nearly. Specifically, each measure begins by bending up to a chord tone. (Actually, this bend precedes each measure by a half beat—a device known as "anticrusis.") After this first chord tone, the second note is in fact a passing diatonic scale tone, followed by the remaining chord tones as the figure descends in arpeggio format. Here's how it plays out: Over D we have the notes D–C–A–F–D (root–♭7–5–♭3–root); over G we have the notes D–C–B♭–G–D (5–4–♭3–root–5); over C we have the notes E–D–C–G–E (3–2–root–5–3); and over A we get chromatically rising unison bends.

The solo enters "phase 3" at measure 33 with its fast single-string picking. Again, let's first consider "what lies beneath:" the same chords, D–G–C–A. Don't see any chords? Well, not overtly. Guitar 1 is actually picking single notes in the slash notation above the staff. Taken together, however, they form chords. Measures 33–34 are a D5 (except the last note, which transitions to the next chord). Measures 35–36 are G5, measures 37–38 are C5, and measures 39–40 rock on a palm-muted A root note (implying an A chord).

Now for the lead finale! The picking speed isn't too difficult to come by if you work at it for a while, because it's all on a single string. Keep a downstroke on all downbeats and gradually push it up. The trouble spot that is most likely to arise is a lack of synchronization between the right and left hands. This is largely due to the fact that although we are picking in groups of fours (sixteenths), the left hand is playing only *three* different notes—the last note in each group is played twice. To improve synchronization, you might try alternating back and forth between playing a measure as it is written, then play it again with only the first three sixteenths of each beat (with a down/up/down picking pattern for each beat). This puts a greater focus on the left hand's job. Then, when you go back to picking all the notes, that hand should "tow the line" a bit better.

The notes simply rise step-wise up the diatonic D minor scale beginning on A (D's 5th). Over G, the lead raises the pattern up by one scale tone, placing the first note on B♭ (G's minor 3rd). Over C, it moves up again, placing the first note on C (the root). At measures 39–40 it comes skipping down, bouncing between the upper, descending scale tones and an open high E string. After peaking on A (root), it comes down the scale (except that F is sharped, lending a brighter quality) throughout measure 39, then turning chromatic through measure 40. The entire sequence then repeats.

After a second time around, the descending phrase is extended, hanging on A for an extra eight measures (measures 41–49). The featured part fills this with an entirely "slippery" chromatic approach. Also of particular interest here is the harmony part of guitar 3. In measure 41, we begin with a high A (above Gtr. 2's E), pegging the chord tones of A5. Then it descends to make 3rds over Gtr. 2's chromatic tones. In measure 42, it plays in unison. In measure 43, the harmony jumps up a minor 3rd and moves in parallel with the chromatic lead part. In measure 44, it again joins in unison.

After all this classically-influenced extravagance, Blackmore is ready to contrast it with a sprinkling of good blues licks—just so you don't forget what you're dealing with here! The final measures 45–49 are squarely in the A blues scale (A–C–D–E♭–E–G).

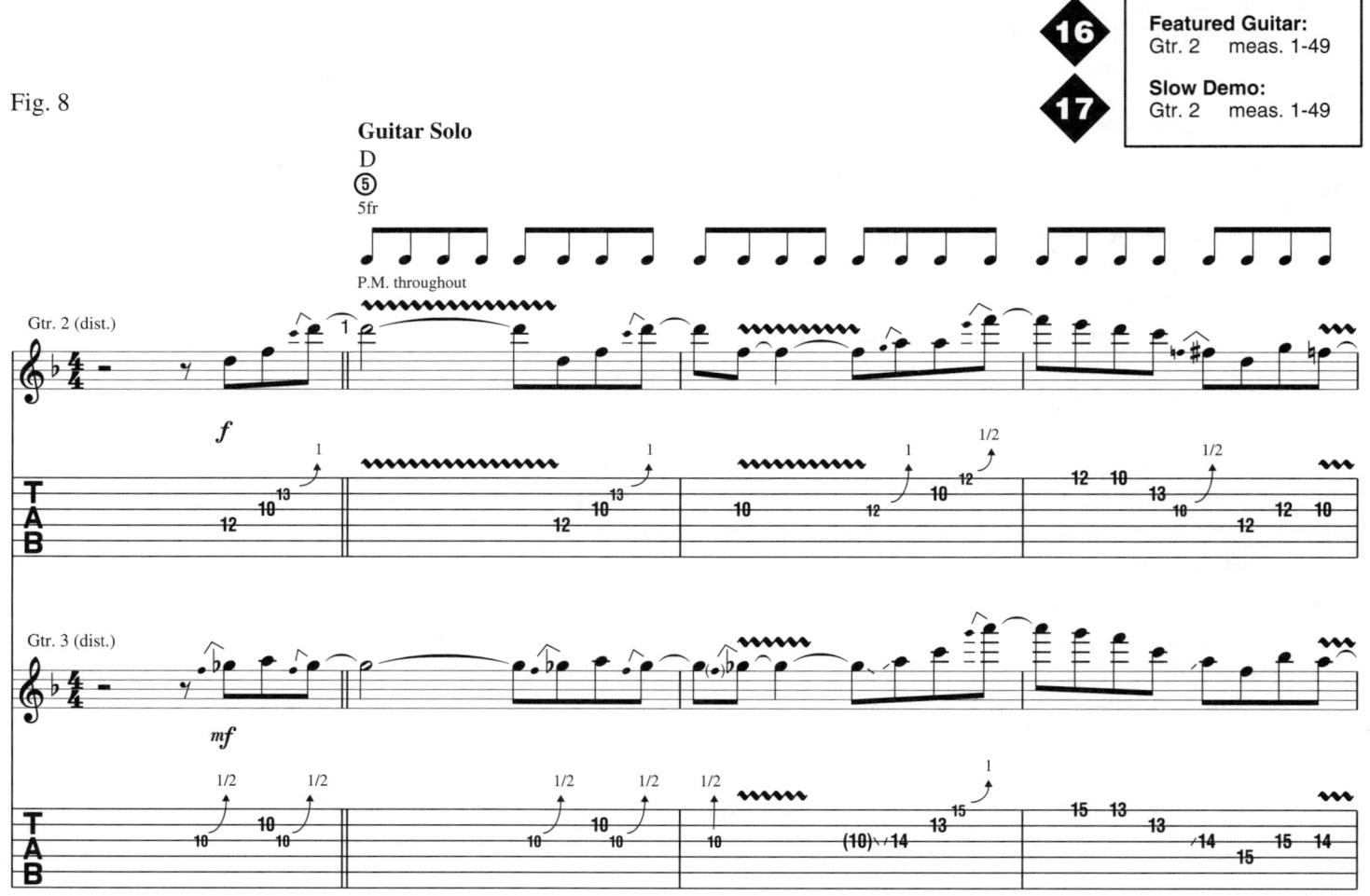

Fig. 8

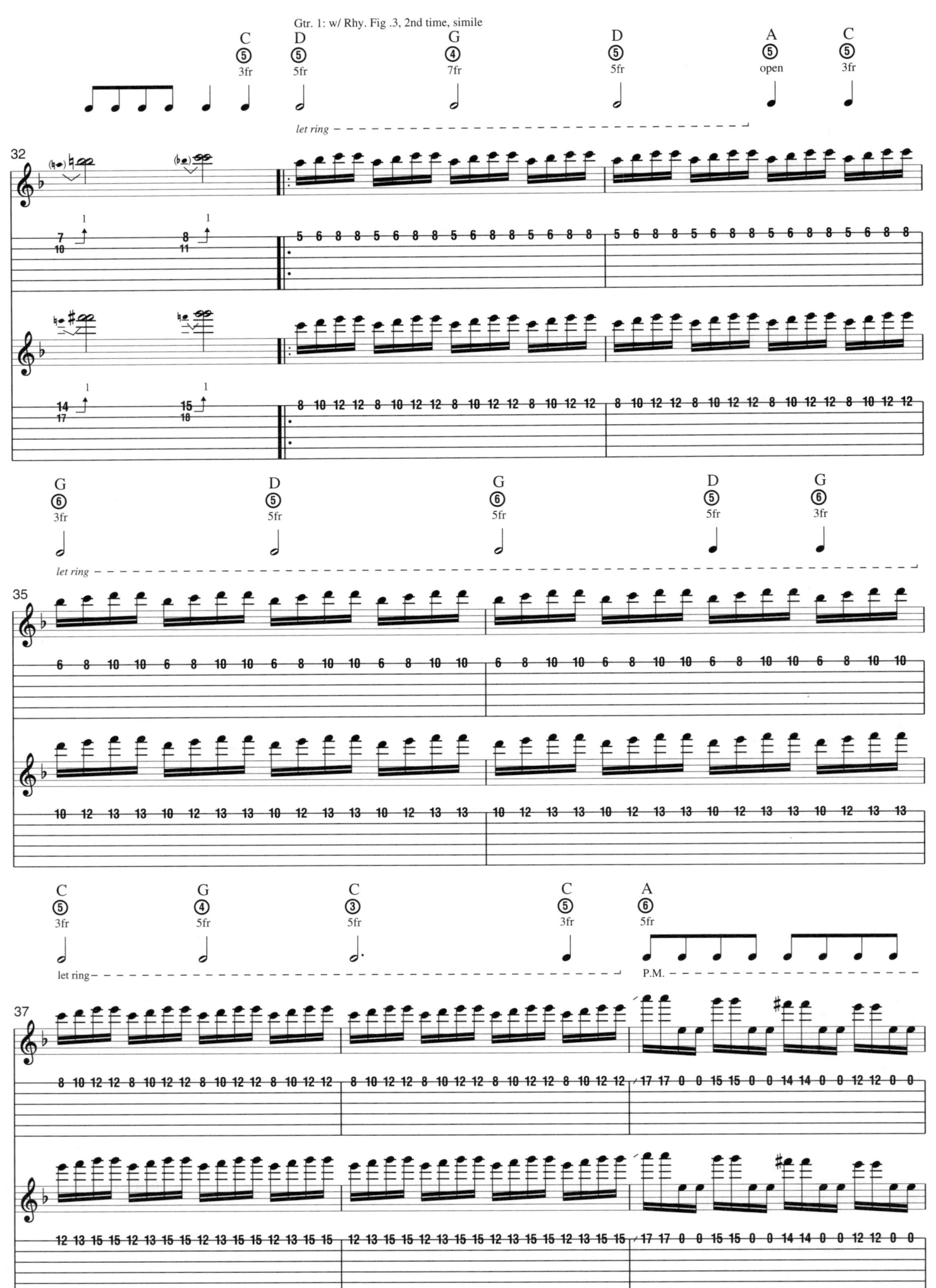

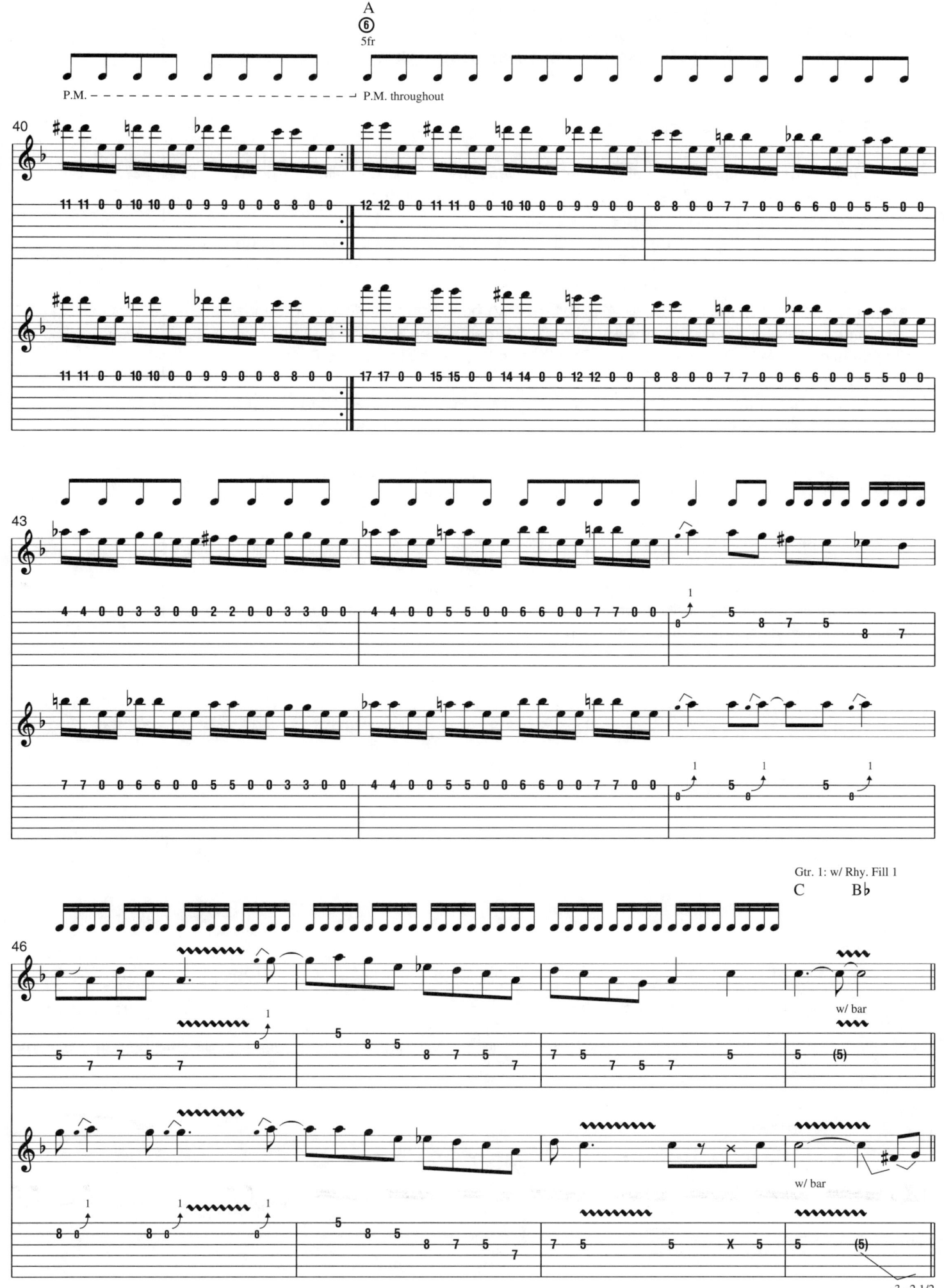

SPACE TRUCKIN'

Words and Music by Ritchie Blackmore, Ian Gillan, Roger Glover, Jon Lord and Ian Paice

Figure 9–Intro, Verse, Pre-Chorus, Chorus

"Space Truckin'" is another cut off *Machine Head* that brings a familiar, reminiscing smile to fans remembering a simpler decade gone by; a fun tune, with no great deep meaning, but one heck of a killer chorus riff!

The guitar enters at the verse with sixth comping chords in a plodding, straightforward rhythm that punches on each downbeat. The progression is Am for two measures (i chord), then a measure of C–D (bIII–IV), and a return to Am on measure four. From measure 25, we see the progression D–A–D–E (IV–I–IV–V) build up to the following chorus. An extra measure of E draws upon the V chord's harmonic tension even further before finally releasing to the tonic at measure 30. The change to E7 (with the added D note) also helps create a stronger pull.

The chorus is based on a strong one-measure, single-note idea. The riff begins with A–E (1–5), then descending chromatic tones take over and it falls to Eb–D (b5–4). Next, the descent continues with C–B–Bb (b3–2–b2) and leans right down into A again to repeat the process. The implied harmonic attribute is Am. Use fifth-position fingering throughout. That is, your index finger takes every note in the fifth fret, your middle finger takes every note in the sixth fret, your ring finger takes every note in the seventh fret, and your pinky finger takes the C note at the eighth fret.

After four measures, the riff shifts down a 4th interval to function as an Em— harmonically speaking, the V chord. The fingering is different, of course, as we are now in the open position. A chromatic walk-up in measure 37 mirrors and counterbalances the descending chromatics, pulling things back up to A.

© 1972 (Renewed 2000) B. FELDMAN & CO. LTD. trading as HEC MUSIC
All Rights for the United States and Canada Controlled and Administered by GLENWOOD MUSIC CORP.
All Rights Reserved   International Copyright Secured   Used by Permission

Figure 10–Bridge, Chorus, Guitar Solo

The bridge is really a modified third verse. Here the guitar fills space with chucking sixth-string harmonics. Place your ring finger at fret 5, but don't press down. Picking this will sound an E harmonic, two octaves above the open string. Now go ahead and rest your middle finger behind it, also on the sixth string. The presence of another finger will tend to make it sound more like a muted click than a pure, natural harmonic—yet it still has an E pitch to it. Your index finger is available to nail the C/E dyads on beat 4 of most measures.

Notice the structural modifications from the original verse. Here we see the original four-measure progression Am–Am–C5–D5–Am applied four times, rather than just two, and the D–A–D–E build has been omitted. Instead, a different build-up tactic is employed. Notice how the last Am chord of the sequence is missing, replaced by E (the V chord). A chromatic walk-up in the fourth measure signals the approaching chorus, and its coincident resolution to the tonic (Am).

The chorus is identical to before, and just as freaking cool to hear and play as the first time around. (The true test of a riff's strength: On repetition, it not only maintains interest, it actually feels stronger!)

The guitar solo happens over a breakdown. That is, the energy level drops dramatically, leaving a kind of musical "hole." Here, Blackmore switches to a thick, bluesy tone employing the neck pickup. The key is Am and the entire solo actually takes place in the common A minor pentatonic box 1 shape. Uncommon phrasing, however, is the key element here that sets it apart. As we have seen before, Blackmore obscures the more typical two-measure and four-measure "break points" that naturally lie between phrases.

Measure 28 kicks things off with a simple three-note motif in A minor pentatonic. Use your middle finger with index tucked behind it for the full-step bend up from C to D. The following three notes briefly paraphrase the original. Then measure 29 begins the answer to the "question" stated in those first six notes. Notice, however, that the answer rolls right on through to the end of measure 30, creating an odd, three-measure phrase in total.

Measure 31 begins a new idea. Pick each E/A dyad with an upstroke and each intervening note-slide combination begins with a downstroke. The lick continues by descending in a staccato-inflected style. Notice the classically derived repeating-tone idea—holding the D note steady while the upper voice falls (oblique motion). This phrase also lasts roughly three measures.

Measure 34 wraps it up, leaving a measure of space to round out the full eight-measure solo. This bit of fluently articulated blues mastery uses—not surprisingly—the A blues scale (A–C–D–E♭–E–G). The sixteenth triplet is the source of rhythmic interest here.

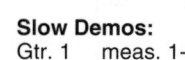

Fig. 10

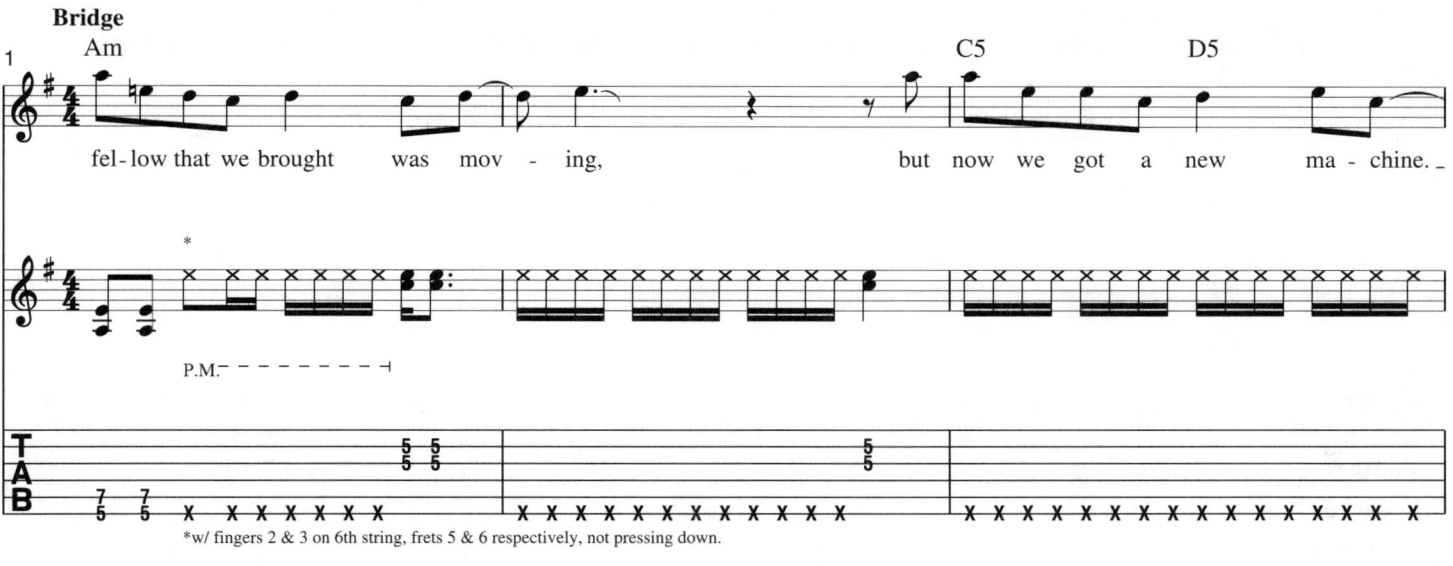

*w/ fingers 2 & 3 on 6th string, frets 5 & 6 respectively, not pressing down.

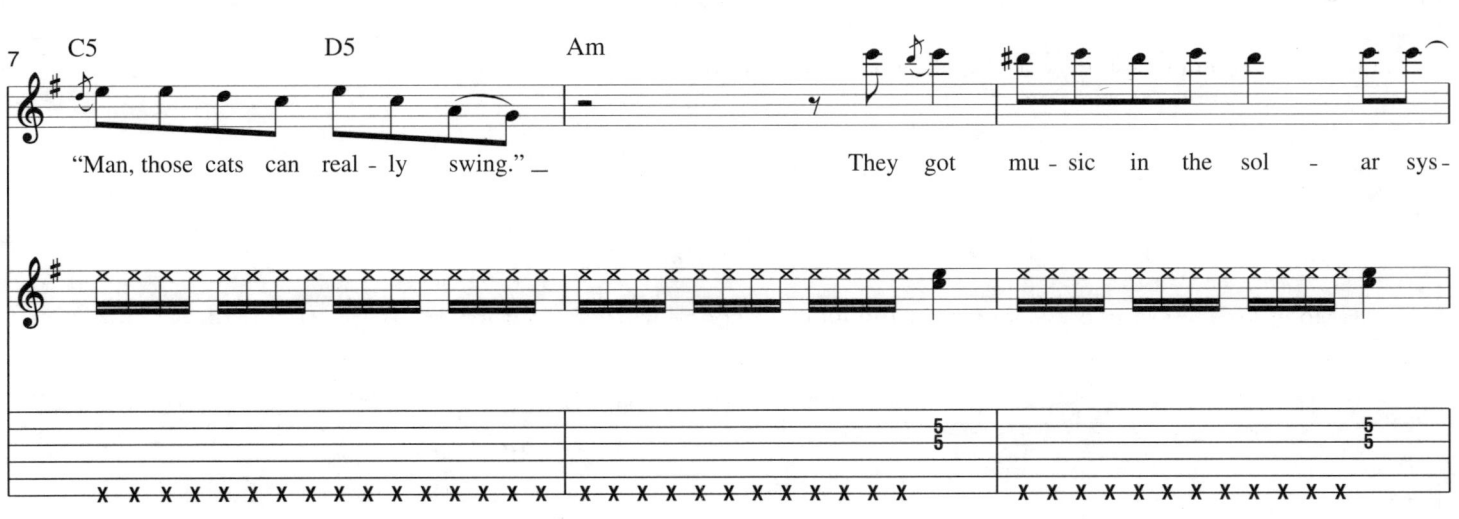

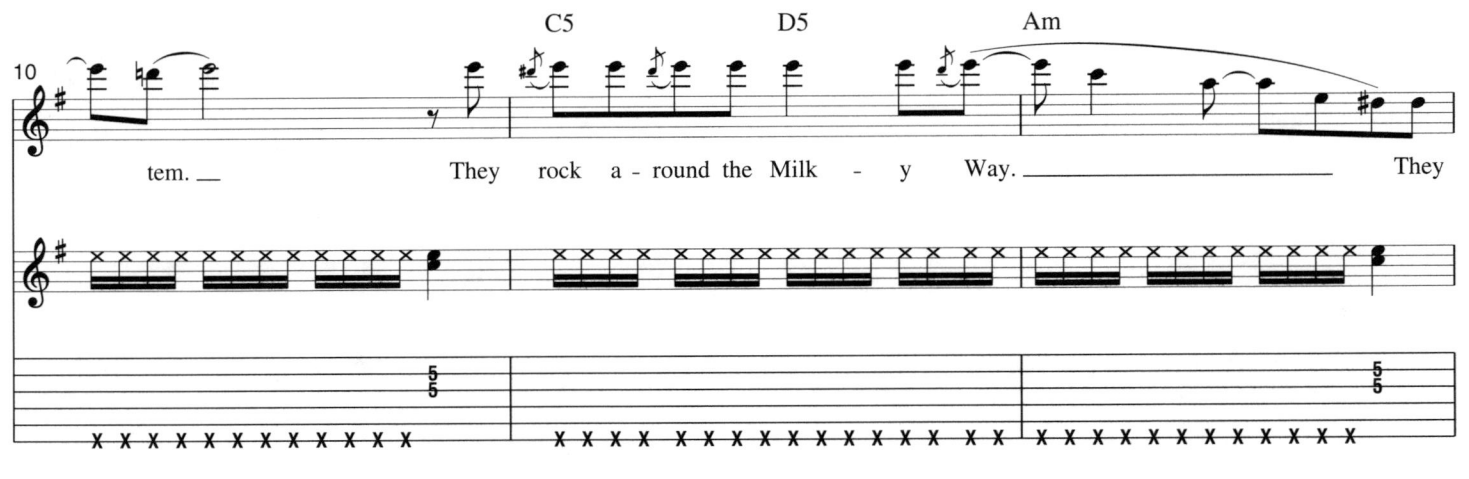

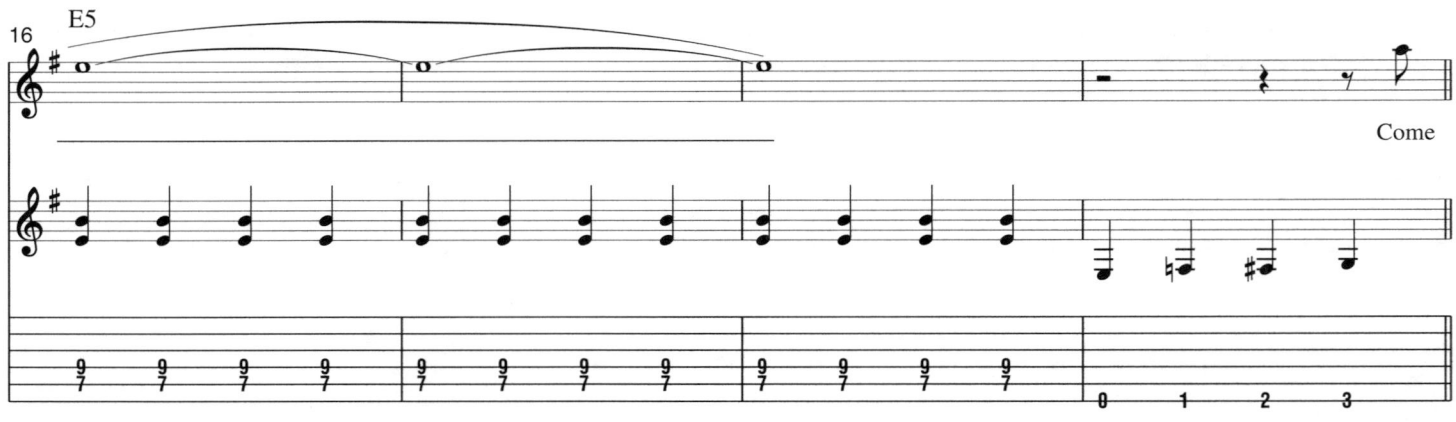
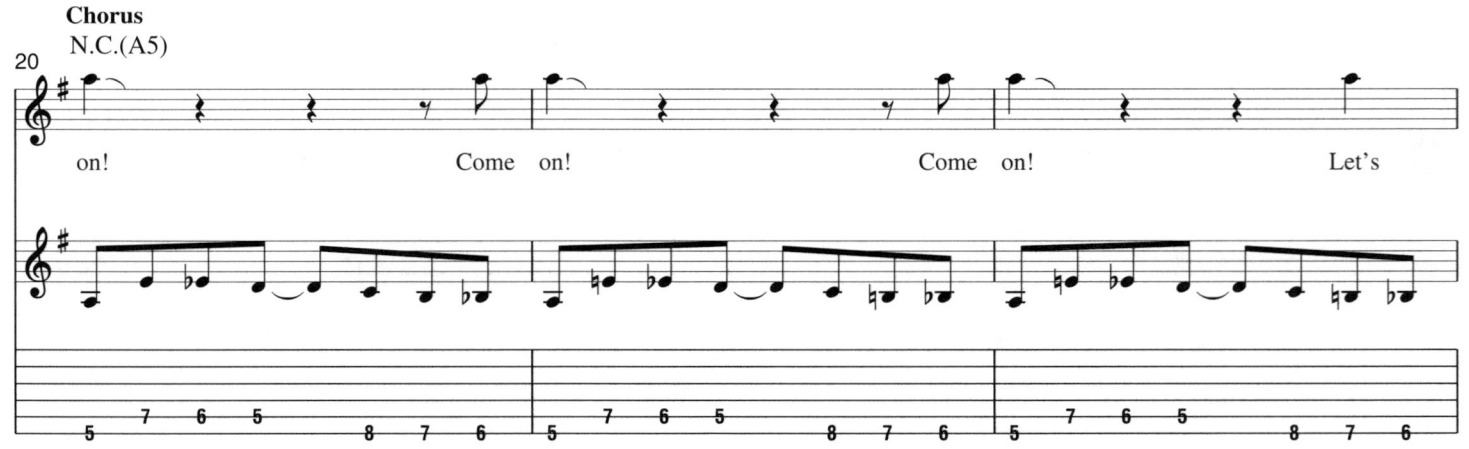

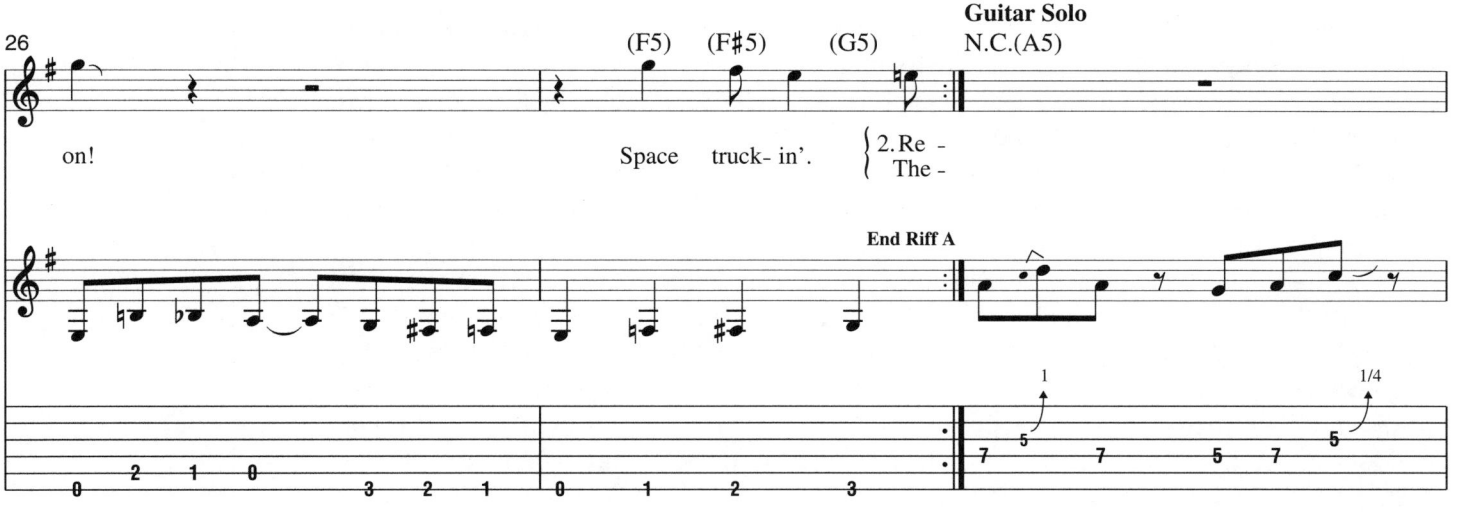

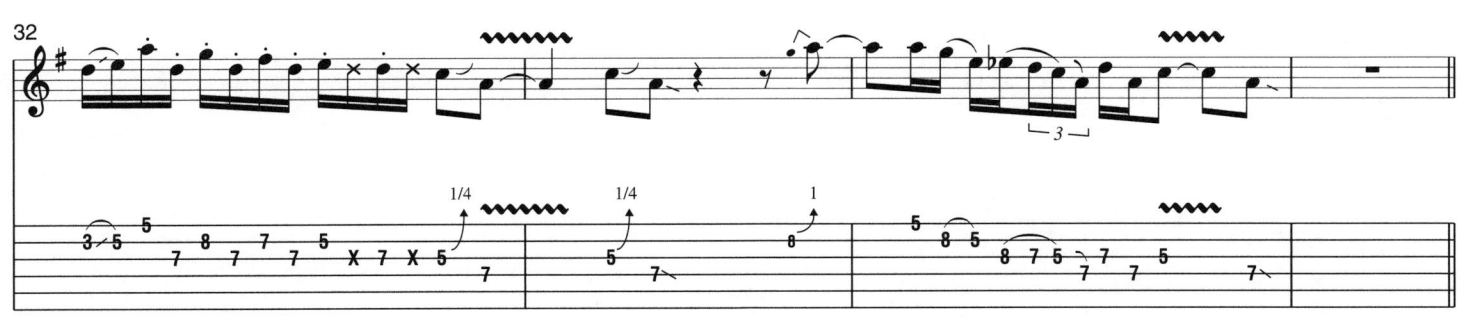

SMOKE ON THE WATER

Words and Music by Ritchie Blackmore, Ian Gillan, Roger Glover, Jon Lord and Ian Paice

Figue 11–Intro and Verse

More than any other, this is the song—no, the *riff*—that launched Deep Purple into the hearts and minds of a generation. Certainly one of the most emulated riffs of all time, to many it is the very embodiment of 1970s hard rock. It may come as somewhat of a shock, then, to realize that the band actually wasn't particularly excited about the song at first. Unaware of its potential, Deep Purple hardly played it live in 1972, and it was overlooked as a single. ("Never Before" was chosen as the first single from *Machine Head* for European release, and an edited version of "Lazy" was picked for the U.S. single.) It wasn't until 1973 that it was released as a single in the U.S., after which time the tune quickly gathered momentum and rose to ultimately become an international rock anthem.

It actually tells the story of the recording of the album, *Machine Head*. The band was scheduled to record the album at a venue called the Casino in Montreux, Switzerland, using the Rolling Stones' 16-track mobile recording studio. But during a concert held there by Frank Zappa and the Mothers of Invention shortly before recording was to commence, someone had fired a flare gun at the ceiling, igniting and burning the Casino to the ground. (In fact, the members of Deep Purple were there in the audience.) The band ended up renting the Grand Hotel, which was closed for the winter season, and the recording began in December 1971.

The song's genesis occurred in the mind of bassist Roger Glover. As he explained in an interview in 1996, "Actually, it [the title] came to me in a sort of dream one or two mornings after the fire. I was alone in my bed…in that mystical time between deep sleep and awakening, when I heard my own voice say those words out loud. I woke up then and asked myself if I actually did say them out loud, and I came to the conclusion that I did. I pondered upon it and realized that it was a potential song title." Later, when the band was together, Roger had the image of smoke spreading out over Lake Geneva in his mind, and put forth the line "smoke on the water." Ian Gillan at first dismissed it, thinking it would be regarded as a drug song. But then, Ritchie suddenly came up with the riff and the song was born. "All I know is that I have always listened to my random thoughts ever since," says Roger.

The famous riff that brought it all together utilizes 4th dyad power chords throughout. Pick with upstrokes to favor the higher root note, or, if you choose to play with downstrokes, make certain that you strike both strings with equal strength. (If the lower of the two notes stands out, it won't sound right.) The root movement of the dyads in the riff spells out the lowest four tones of the G blues scale (G–B♭–C–D♭–D–F). To get the right feel for it, pay attention not just to the timing of when to sound the notes, but just as importantly, exactly when to stop the strings (for the rests).

The verse simply arpeggiates a three-string G5 power chord repetitively, dipping to F5 for a moment in the middle of measure 8. Notice that this pretty much follows the now-familiar Deep Purple formula for most progressions: Four-measure phrases starting and ending on the tonic, moving elsewhere in each third measure.

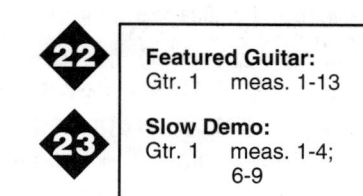

Figure 12–Chorus

The chorus begins on C, the IV chord, sounding relatively brighter. Then we get the darkness of the powerful leaning tone, A♭ (♭II). This resolves to G, where the guitar simply allows octaves to ring while the bass and organ grind out a G minor pentatonic groove underneath. These two measures on G (measures 3–4) also act as a breathing space between the "active" measures 1–2, and together create a full four-measure phrase.

The next phrase begins with another C–A♭ (IV–♭II), but cuts directly into the riff, which effectively functions as a Gm tonic (i) chord. By leaving out the naturally anticipated breathing space on the second time around, the riff seems to jump in somewhat unexpectedly at that point, and thereby drive the song forward a bit harder.

24 Featured Guitar: Gtr. 1 meas. 1-13

25 Slow Demo: Gtr. 1 meas. 1-4

Figure 13–Guitar Solo

At first appearance it seems that the solo works over a verse progression—it has a similar rhythmic treatment and consists of arpeggiated power chords, starting with G5. Look closer, however, and you'll find the progression is altered: G5–G5–C5–G5 (i–i–iv–i).

Over this, the lead begins in the box 4/box 5 area of G minor pentatonic. Variety is achieved primarily through careful articulation. Notice that the first full-step bend is actually a pre-bend. Also, each of the B♭ (♭3rd) notes in measure 2 are given a little "twist"—bluesy quarter-tone bends.

In measure 3, over C, Blackmore continues in the G minor pentatonic box 5 pattern, but gives a slight nod to the underlying chord motion, reinforcing it by virtue of bending B♭ up to C (root). A nice finger vibrato sustains it. He then goes diatonic (G natural minor) in the remainder of measures 3–4, playing staccato style.

This melody steps seamlessly over the phrase demarcation into measure 5 without ever breaking stride. Pay particular attention here to the series of pre-bends. Then notice how they are used motivically, repeated in the next measure but at a different pitch level. At measure 7, Ritchie this time follows the progression to Cm—actually shifting up to C minor pentatonic box 1 at eighth position for a full-fledged C blues lick. Yet, in beat 4, he manages to wind his way back to G, diatonically. Relative to the tonic, G, these notes can be seen as being G natural minor. Relative to the underlying C5 at that point, they form C Dorian. Measure 8 is back in Gm territory without reservation, working the G natural minor scale in a melodic, upward sequence.

Measure 9 is the start of the third phrase. And true to form, Blackmore again completely obliterates it. The result is a wandering, ongoing feeling without any clear boundaries. Over the C5 move at measure 11, he chooses the opposite tact from the approach utilized over the previous C5. This time he ignores it, playing straight on through it in G minor pentatonic box 1. (As Cm is in the key of Gm, all the notes of G minor will work over the Cm chords as well.)

Measures 13–14 rise up into the box 2 area of G minor pentatonic. At measure 15 it's back to Cm in the eighth position, then climbing diatonically to D (G's 5th).

The progression now opens up to sustaining C5 (iv) and then F5 (♭VII) power chords before plunging back headlong into the infamous riff. Over these chords, the lead waxes majestic. At first glance, the pattern formed in measures 17–18 may seem to look like D minor pentatonic box 1. But in reality, it's a G minor pentatonic box 4 shape, applied over the iv chord. Over ♭VII, the answer is a G minor pentatonic box 1 in measure 19, box 2 in measure 20.

The often-emulated, gradually releasing reverse-bend technique takes over at measures 21–22. After falling a full whole step, Blackmore resolves with a final bend from F (♭7th) to G (root), sustaining with finger vibrato as the omnipotent riff powers on into history.

WOMAN FROM TOKYO

Words and Music by Ritchie Blackmore, Ian Gillan, Roger Glover, Jon Lord and Ian Paice

Figure 14–Intro, Verse and Chorus

By the time *Who Do We Think We Are?* was tracked in 1973, Ritchie Blackmore and Ian Gillan were reportedly "at each other's throats" on a fairly regular basis. Yet, they managed to crank out at least one more powerhouse hit before parting ways, with "Woman From Tokyo." Released in the U.S. as a single that same year, it rose quickly into *Billboard's* Top 100. Blackmore later mentioned that the memorable main riff was actually his rendition of an Eric Clapton idea—from the song "Cat's Squirrel."

This riff requires hybrid picking, that is, a combination of pick and fingers. Hold the pick between your thumb and index finger; this takes the low E note. This should also be slightly palm muted. The higher strings 3 and 4 are plucked with your available middle and ring fingers of the picking hand. Striking the strings perfectly simultaneously like this has a distinctly different quality than the more standard guitar picking technique, wherein one string is always struck slightly before the next as the pick is dragged across.

Musically speaking, we are in the key of E major. The main riff appears here in the entrance in a somewhat relaxed presentation, relative to its appearance later in the song. After a low E pegs the tonal center, an E–A (root–4th) dyad suggests Esus4. Use your middle and ring fingers, respectively, keeping your first finger available for the upcoming G♯. The higher note of the two, A, then pulls off to G♯ (major 3rd) at the first fret. Next, the opening note/dyad pattern repeats, more or less, but with a different rhythmic treatment. Low E now enters on beat 3 and lasts just an eighth note. The following dyads E/A and E/G♯ follow, both on upbeats. At the second measure, upbeat of 2, we get back to the tonic chord with a B/E dyad. Technically, this is a 4th dyad power chord. Then an E minor pentatonic-style lick rises up to hang on D (♭7th) for two full measures, giving the riff plenty of breathing space and rounding out a four-measure phrase.

The riff repeats in measures 9–12 with a different ending. This time, Ritchie takes the 4th dyad E5 power chord and shifts up chromatically to F5, F♯5, then settling on G5 (♭III), performing full three-string power chords on F♯5 and G5. The salient feature here lies in the rhythm, with its strangely staggered quality. At first this may seem to be based on a quarter-note triplet rhythm. But upon closer inspection, we see that it's actually a sixteenth-based rhythm. Each note/rest combination lasts exactly three fourths of a beat—the equivalent of three sixteenths.

At measure 13, we have an interlocking combination. Each instrument—guitar, bass, and organ—takes a different tact. Each is a simple part, but taken together they support one another and create an interesting, composite texture. Measures 15–16 function as an "ending tag," extending an extra two measures with a quick pull-off lick and vibrato bar treatment. The sustaining chord here is actually an E minor without the root. This leaves a G/B (♭3/5) dyad, with added open B string in unison.

The band finally kicks into high gear on the full riff at measure 17. Here, the original idea presented earlier is shortened to its two-measure core and repeated, with a different ending. This has the effect of giving us the quicker-paced energy of two-measure phrasing while still preserving the overall four-measure phrase length.

Measure 24 employs a chromatic walk-up as a means to get from E up to G (♭III) for the verse. (Use of chromatics in this way is clearly a Deep Purple trademark, and can also be seen in "Highway Star," "Space Truckin'," and the bass lines of "Smoke on the Water," as well as later songs such as "Burn.")

The verse juxtaposes a G major tonality against the preceding E major (actually E7, or Mixolydian). We can easily hear that these keys must somehow be related, by virtue of their seamless transition. But how? E major doesn't even have a G in it—it uses G♯. The answer is that G is the relative major of the parallel minor. In other words, take E major and swap it with E minor (blending parallel major and minor is a common rock and blues practice). Now from the perspective of E minor, G major is right at home, as ♭III. Listen for this interesting tonality shift.

The verse itself maintains a bass pedal tone of G throughout. Over this, the guitar strikes a series of clanging, pendulum-like suspensions, swinging between G and various types of F/G ("F over G") chords. The chorus enters at measure 33, utilizing the riff established in measures 17-24.

BURN

Words and Music by Ritchie Blackmore, David Coverdale, Jon Lord and Ian Paice

Figure 15–Intro, Verse and Interlude

After vocalist Ian Gillan and bassist Roger Glover left the band, Deep Purple recruited the talents of David Coverdale and Glenn Hughes to forge ahead. The initial result of "Deep Purple Mark III" was *Burn*, released the following year, 1974. The album proved to be a strong comeback, showing that the band still had a lot more to offer.

The title track is a fast-paced, high-energy rocker in the key of Gm. Blackmore uses his characteristic "thumb over the top of the neck" technique (à la Hendrix) in the main riff to hold down the low G. Over this, sliding 4th dyad power chords indicate B♭5–A5 (♭III–II), and a stab up to C (IV). The one-measure motif is then repeated, rhythmically displaced—each note is pushed forward in time by one half beat. The riff builds the form "ABAC," producing a four-measure phrase in which measures 1 and 3 are the same and measures 2 and 4 incorporate alternate endings.

The verse is based on the progression Gm–F/G–Gm–C7, with two measures per chord. This is in fact fairly similar to the harmonic underpinnings seen in the verse of the previous song, until the final chord (except that G is minor in this case). Blackmore treats it differently, however, with simple octaves. Notice also the characteristic chromatics, used as a transitional device between chords.

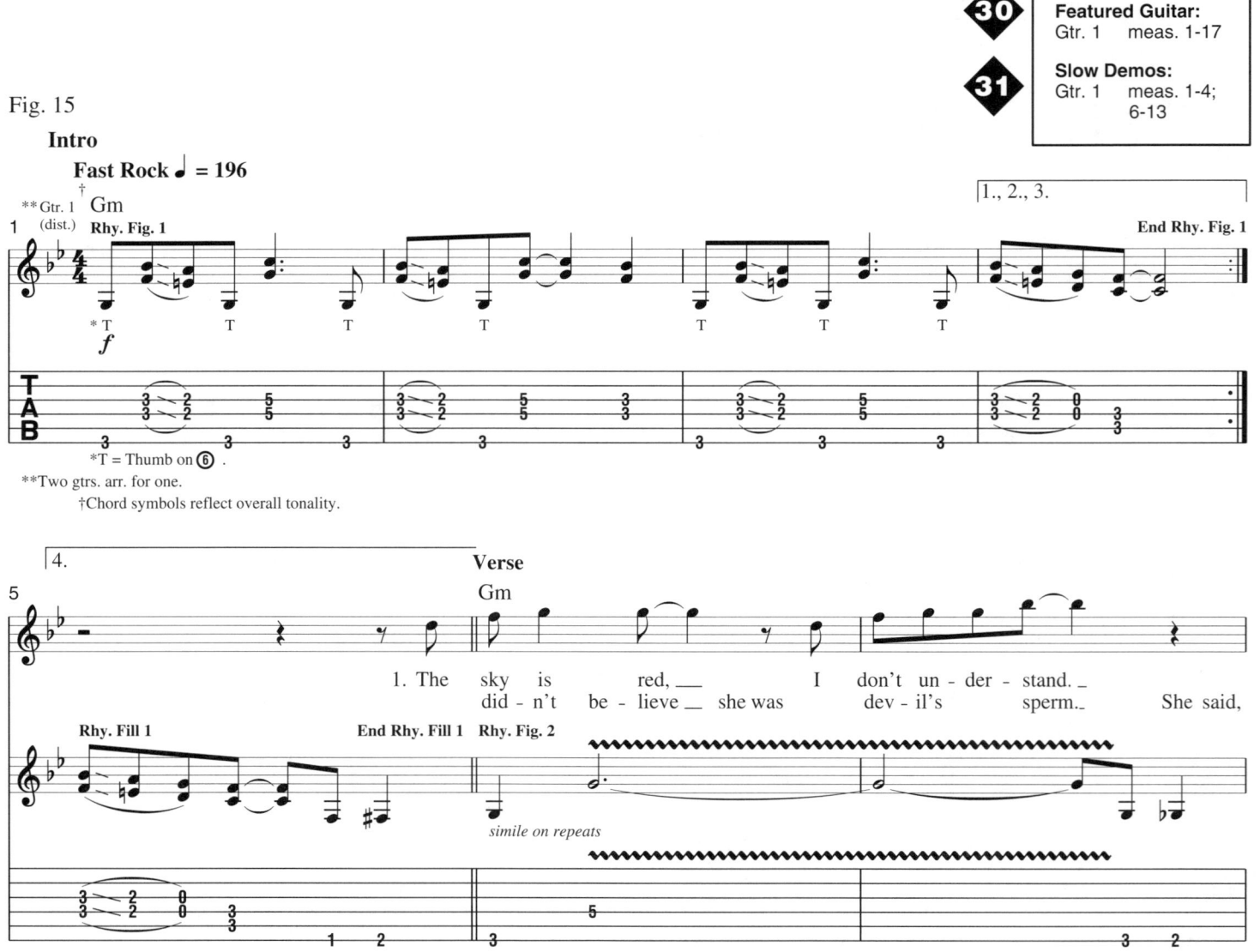

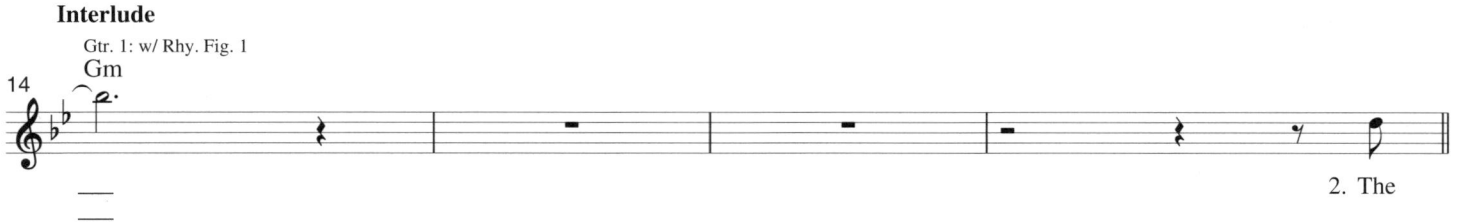

Figure 16–Guitar Solo

The solo of "Burn" takes the composed classical influence of "Highway Star" one step further, with its two clean-tone guitars working together in harmony through a maze of arpeggios.

The progression is arranged in an eight-measure sequence: Gm–Cm–F–B♭ (i–iv–♭VII–♭III), then E♭–Cm–D–D (♭VI–iv–V–V). Beginning on the tonic chord, it utilizes the Aeolian modality exclusively, until the final V chord. (Turning major, this creates a temporary G harmonic minor tonality.) Gtrs. 2 and 4 split apart in measures 7–8; while Gtr. 2 rises chromatically from D major's 3rd, to the 4th, ♯4th, then 5th, Gtr. 4 simply holds down the D major chord tones A and F♯ (5th and 3rd). In measures 13–16, a quick i–iv–i–iv–V marks the culmination of the solo.

Featured Guitar:
Gtr. 2 meas. 1-32

Slow Demo:
Gtr. 2 meas. 1-16

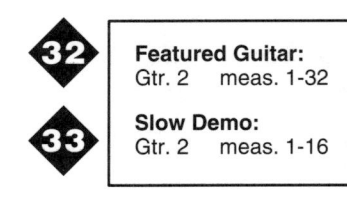

Fig. 16

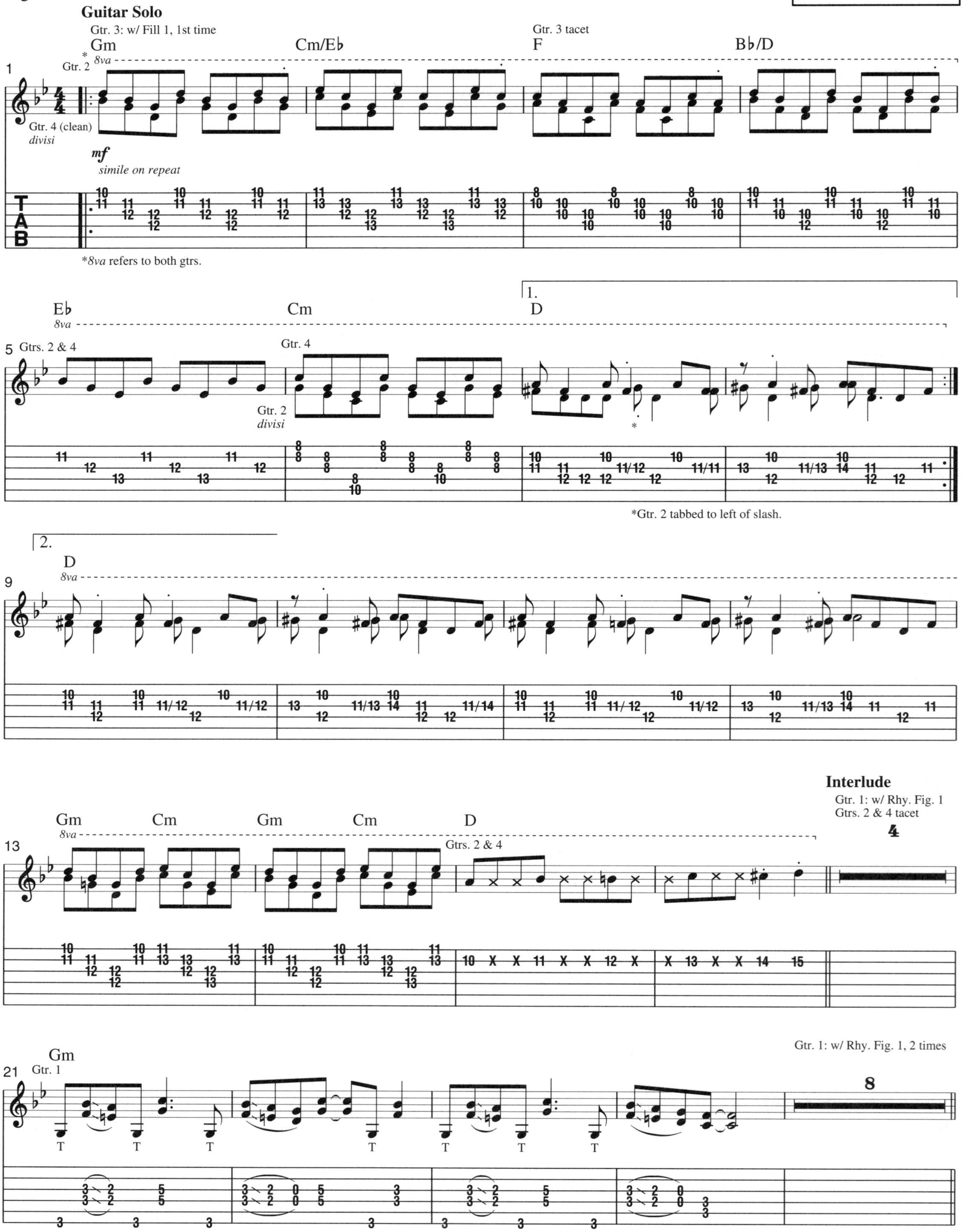

KNOCKING AT YOUR BACK DOOR
Words and Music by Ritchie Blackmore, Ian Gillan and Roger Glover

Figure 17–Intro, Verse, Pre-Chorus and Chorus

After Ritchie Blackmore left the band in 1974, Deep Purple forged on for several years before the members went their separate ways in the later 1970s. At that point, it seemed the "nail was in the coffin," and fans assumed the band was relegated to the annals of history. So it was quite a shock then, in 1984, when Deep Purple suddenly announced the reunion of the band's original "Mark II" lineup, exactly a decade after parting ways.

Their first moments together were reportedly at a conference room in Greenwich, Connecticut. As Jon Lord recalls, "...when we walked into that room, and suddenly these five people were together for the first time in ten years—together—everyone just started smiling. And I think it was Ritchie who said, right then, 'Well, let's do it!'" Deep Purple was renewed, recharged, and as creative as ever. The result: *Perfect Strangers*, released that same year. Powered by the smash hit "Knocking at Your Back Door," the album quickly went multiplatinum. The riff of "Knocking at Your Back Door" works over a relatively static bass line. Rooted in the key of B minor, the bass lays out the root movement of a Bm–Bm–G–A–Bm progression. Notice the same thematic structure seen previously in the verse progression of both "Strange Kind of Woman" and "Space Truckin'"—namely, a four-measure phrase consisting of two measures on the tonic, moving elsewhere for the third measure (subdivided into two halves), then returning to the tonic on measure 4. Harmonically, this is an Aeolian cadence (i–♭VI–♭VII–I), which happens to be a staple heavy-metal idea of the period.

The guitar colors this basic design with a series of chord dyads. On beat 1 we see A/D (♭7th/♭3rd), which—taken together with the bass—creates a Bm7 chord. The next dyad is a major 3rd shape, formed by dropping the upper D note a half step to C♯. Next, it rises to B/E (root/4th), making a temporary Bsus4. Then it falls back down to wrap around and settle on F♯/B (5th/root)—a B5 power chord in 4th dyad form. Continuing with the same power-chord dyad shapes, Blackmore then essentially follows the G–A–Bm portion of the progression. Notice the same rhythmic motif used throughout, in the form of the repeated eighth-note/dotted quarter-note timing.

Beginning at measure 9, the verse uses accent points and space to provide a contrasting texture to that of the opening riff. The progression is now Bm–D–A, with one measure per chord, followed by G–A sharing a measure. In other words, i–♭III–♭VII, ♭VI–♭VII. This is a purely Aeolian (natural minor) progression.

The pre-chorus features a thicker, melodic backdrop in support of the strong vocal melody, with the guitar playing sparsely. It first opens on the G (♭VI chord), shifts down to E (IV), then moves through a quick alternating D–A sequence. Here, notice how the single-note guitar voice picks out a rising, stepwise melody made up of all chord tones: D (root of D), E (5th of A), F♯ (major 3rd of D), then falling to a low open A. Blackmore embellishes this final A with an A–B trill, harkening back to his classical training as a younger guitarist. Structurally, the main riff in the intro also later functions as the underpinning for the chorus (similar to the approach utilized in "Woman from Tokyo" and "Burn").

34

35

Featured Guitar:
Gtr. 1 meas. 1-50

Slow Demos:
Gtr. 1 meas. 1-4; 9-12; 16; 24-33

Fig. 17

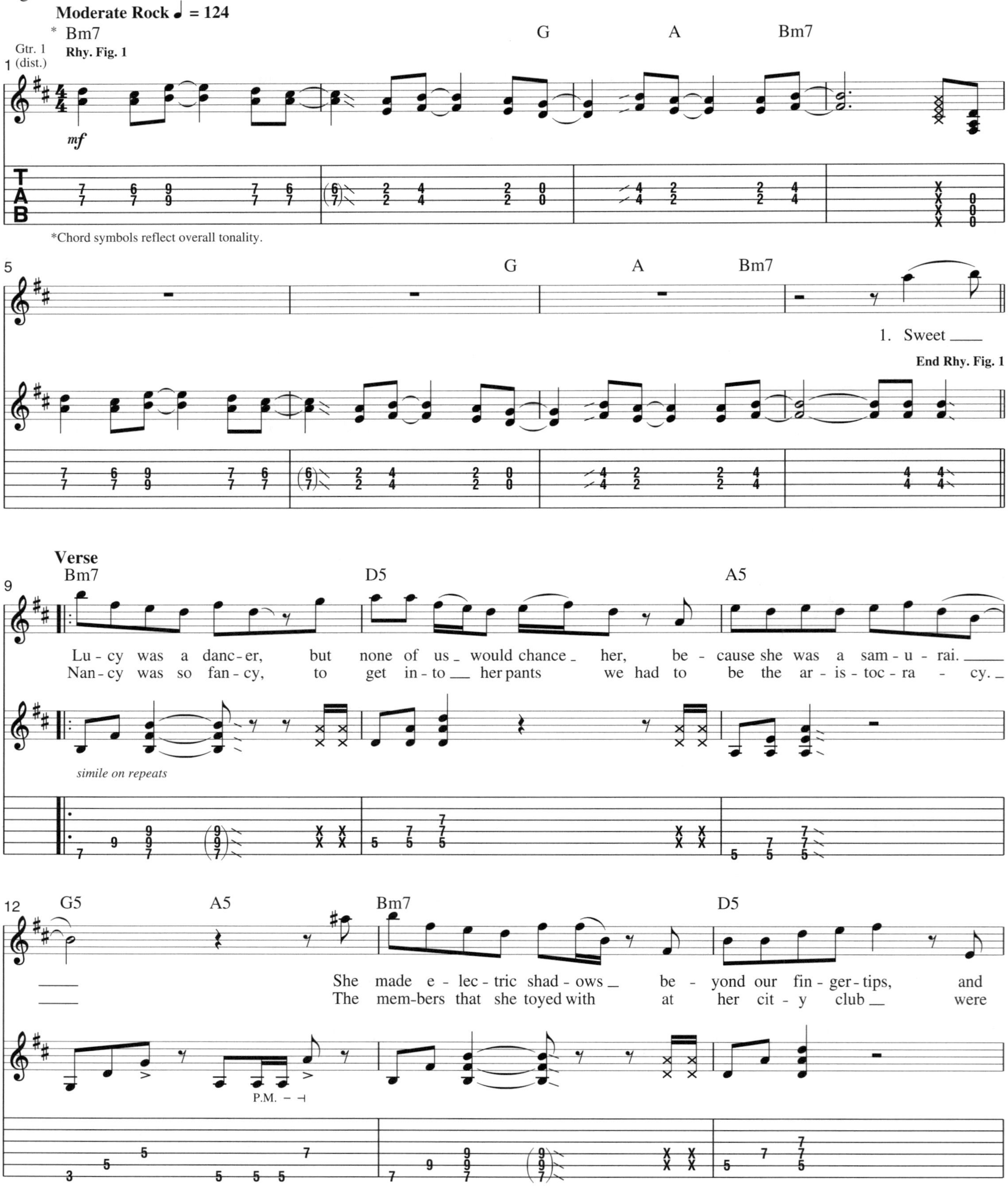

Figure 18–Guitar Solo

This is perhaps one of Ritchie Blackmore's most decisive lead guitar moments; an instant when his style comes together with the perfect blend of technical mastery, phrasing genius, and tonal ferocity.

Based in the key of F# minor, Ritchie opens with a gripping full-step bend and gradual release from A (4th) to B (5th) and back again, in good old box 1 at second position. Heavy picking helps to sharply define and separate the notes that follow, which descend from F# (root) to E (b7th), then turn chromatic with a D# (6th) passing tone added into the otherwise diatonic F# natural minor scale (F#–G#–A–B–C#–D–E). Then it's back to F# blues on beat 4 and continuing on into measure 2.

Nearly a full two beats of pickup notes precede measure 3, firmly establishing the repeated three-note pull-off sequence even before the actual phrase begins. At measure 3, we see an advanced, "compounded rhythm"—that is, the notes may be seen as being grouped together, and these groups themselves make a rhythmic pattern against the underlying beat. (You may recall that we saw this same idea earlier at the beginning of the "Lazy" solo.) Listen for this "deeper" rhythm, marked by the appearance of each B note, played at the fourth fret, third string.

Measure 5 begins diatonically in the F# box 5 area. A quick hammer/pull embellishment of C# (5th) opens the line. Beat 2 starts on A (b3rd), dips pentatonically to F# (root), then just as quickly shoots diatonically back to G#–A (2nd–b3rd). The pull-off to open A is more an accidental feature than by design. In beat 3, he goes thoroughly pentatonic, beginning in the "low extension" of F# minor pentatonic box 4 and then shifting up into standard box 4 at ninth position. A sixteenth-triplet pickup pulls into measure 6 for a fast sextuplet run. Note the strong emphasis (on downbeat 1) of a tense and out-of-key *major* 7th tone. This is finally resolved to the F# at the end of measure 6, albeit at a lower octave. The run skillfully blends diatonic and pentatonic approaches in the F#m box 4 area of the neck.

Ritchie gets downright hostile in the next two bars, attacking the strings in a series of harsh, rhythmic rakes—a brief foreshadowing of the climactic moment yet to come. And after a few bars of bluesy string-bending action in F# minor pentatonic box 1, position fourteen, come it does—in the form of an awesome sweep/rake arpeggio sequence.

This begins at the end of measure 10. Basically, you can regard this as a long "grace-note rake" up to (and over, actually) the high F# note that lies at the beginning of measure 11. Coming down, Blackmore treats it like a fast blues lick. Use an upstroke sweep here. The ending of beat 1 is another downstroke arpeggio rake, culminating with a second high F# at downbeat 3. A quick hammer/pull follows, creating an F#–A–F# (root–b3rd–root) sequence. This also comes down following the blues scale. A third and final sweeping arpeggio reaches F# on the upbeat of 3. Hiding within all these ridiculously fast notes, there is a simpler order to things. It's another compounded rhythm, actually. Listen for the high F#s creating the rhythm pattern: downbeat 1, downbeat 2, and then upbeat of 3.

Perhaps in a nod of acknowledgment of contemporary virtuoso Eddie Van Halen, a wild overbend of two full steps (the equivalent of four frets) comes at us next, raising E (b7th) at the seventeenth fret all the way up and over the root, to G# (2nd). This is followed by a pre-bend and release down. A descending chromatic line then hints back to the solo's opening measure, repeating the tones exactly, but up a full octave in fourteenth (box 1) position. The commonly bent 4th tone (B), located on the third string, comes next. However, rather than the typical whole-step fare, Blackmore continues in "overbending mode" and pushes it an amazing 2 1/2 steps (the equivalent of 5 frets), recalling the feel and technique of Van Halen in the solo of his "You Really Got Me" cover.

The remainder of measure 13 is pure Blackmore, shifting deftly between minor pentatonic and major (at beat 4), then wailing on the bar in trademark fashion in measure 14.

Another classically-inspired minor arpeggio and diatonic embellishment open up measure 15. This is quickly followed by a return to the bluesy minor pentatonic approach. Measure 16 closes by just as quickly reverting back to F♯ natural minor.

At measure 17, Ritchie relaxes the feel a bit and allows some breathing room, perhaps to allow the listener to digest all that has gone before—or, perhaps simply to establish a new, lower-level dynamic from which to build again. (Or both!) Regardless of the reasoning, build again he does, rising through measures 19–20.

Measure 21 begins the final phrase on a high note, literally. In F♯ minor pentatonic box 1, at fourteenth position, Blackmore pushes up to the tonic note, a high F♯, then winds around pentatonically for a bit in the same position for the better part of two measures. Then, one last arpeggio sweep acts as a pickup into the midpoint of the phrase (measure 23). Of interest here is the target note on beat 1, measure 23—G♯, the 9th tone, gives a colorful flavoring. At beat 3, he drops an octave and begins his descent.

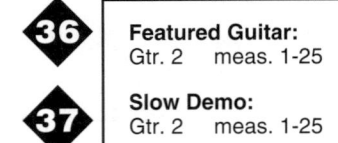

36 Featured Guitar:
Gtr. 2   meas. 1-25

37 Slow Demo:
Gtr. 2   meas. 1-25

Fig. 18

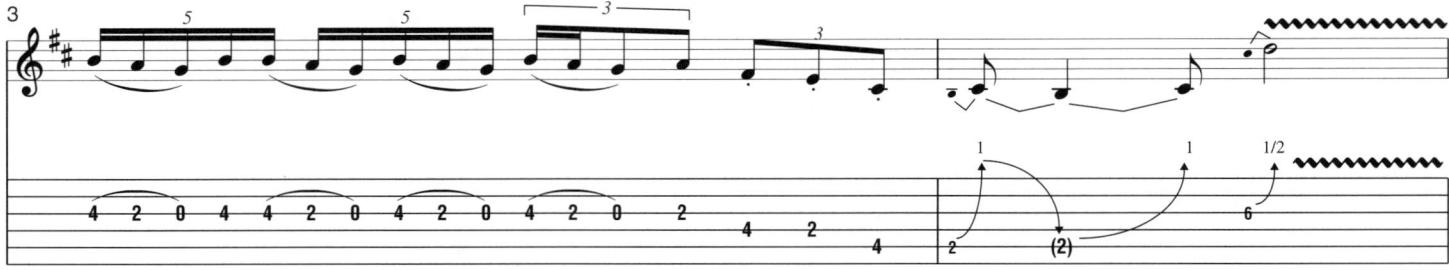

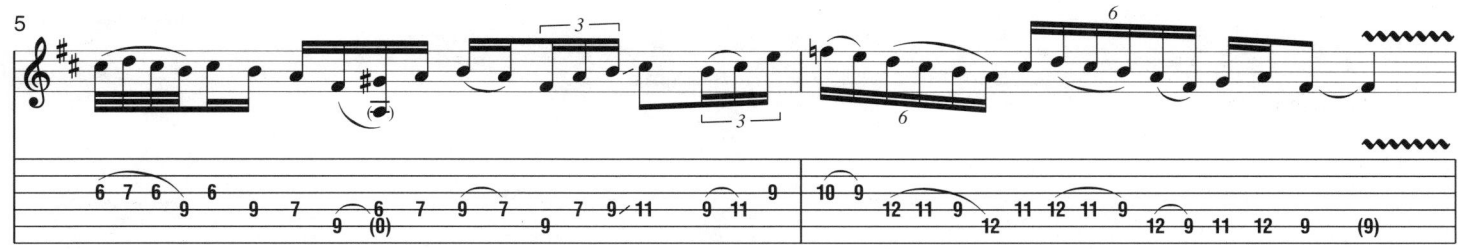
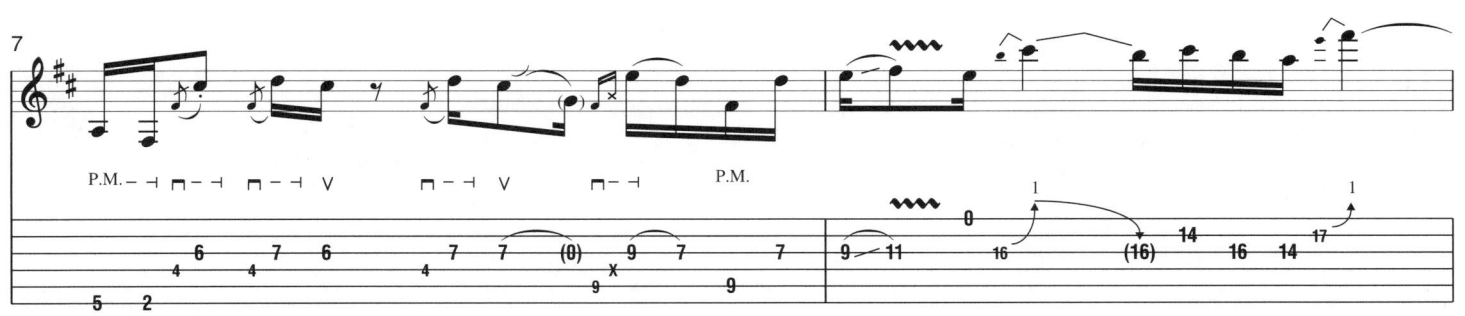
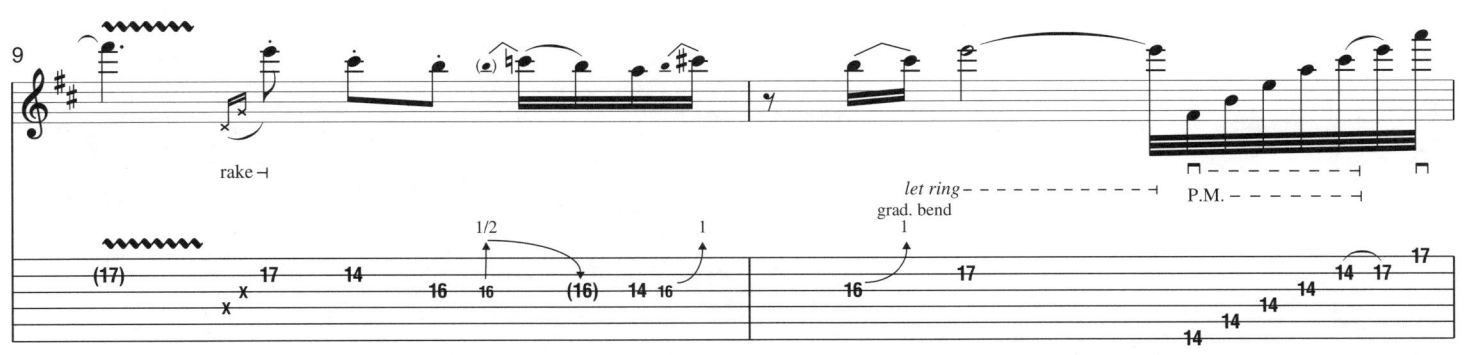
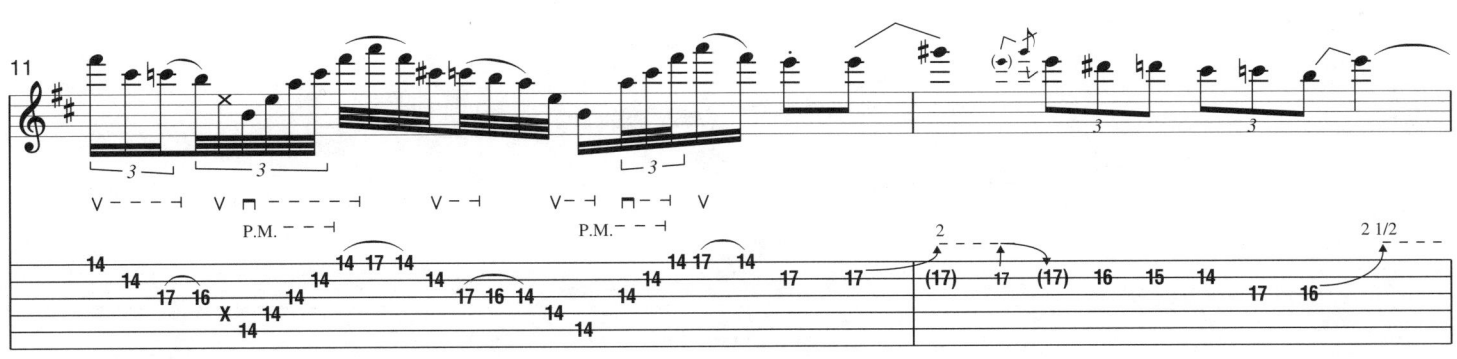
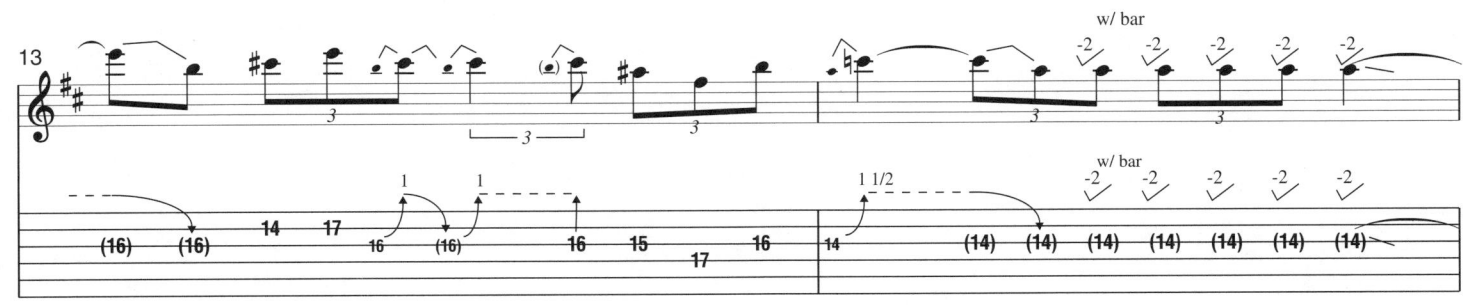

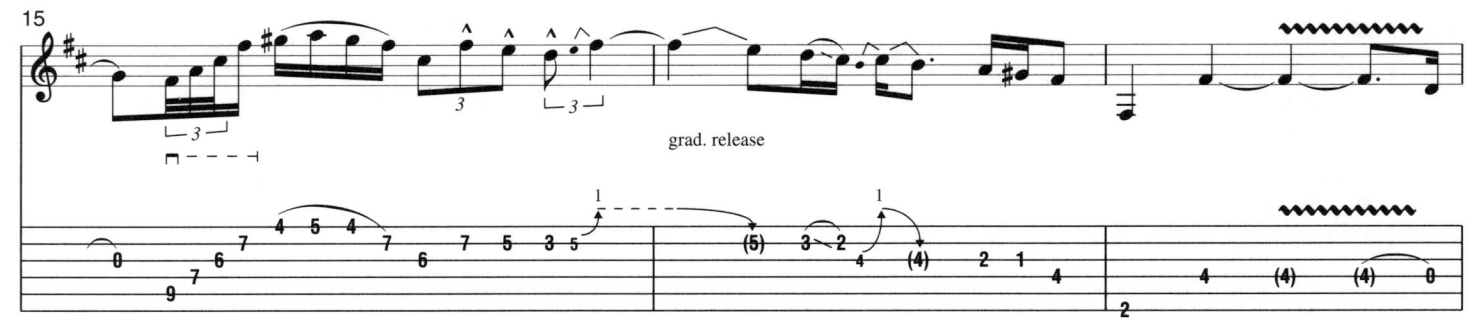
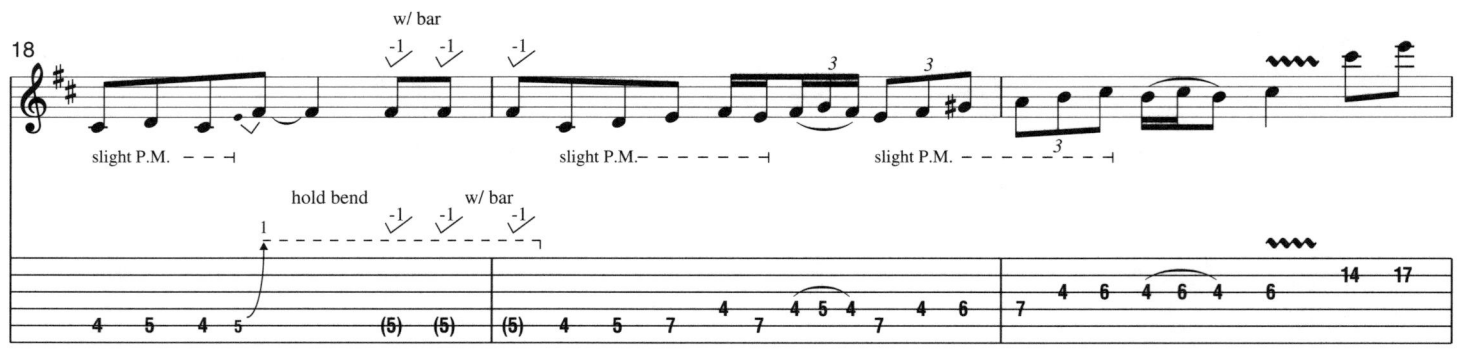
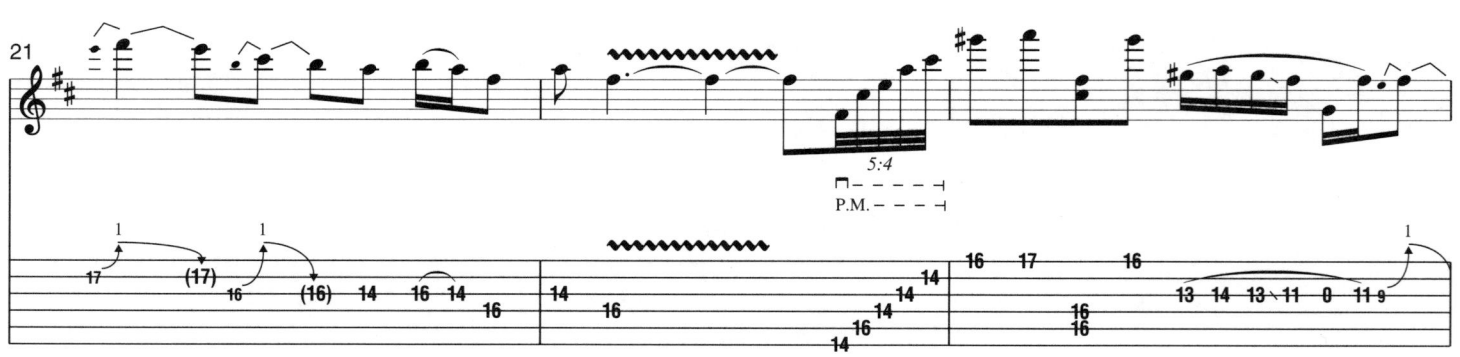

HUSH
Words and Music by Joe South

Figure 19–Intro, Verse, Pre-Chorus and Chorus

This cover song has become a Deep Purple classic, reaching all the way back to the band's earliest moments together (the Mark I lineup, that is). It first appeared on *Shades of Deep Purple* (1968) and was in fact Deep Purple's first single release, which scored a Top 5 hit in the U.S., although it was largely ignored in their home country of England. Twenty years later, the band released an updated version of "Hush" on the live album *Nobody's Perfect* (1988). The same recording also went on a new CD single and EP.

Sparse power chord accents are interspersed with muted left-hand "chucking." This is accomplished by laying several fingers of the left hand lightly across a number of strings, and simultaneously palm muting the other end. When the strings are picked, they produce only a choked, rhythmic "click" with no defined pitch.

The featured guitar part takes Gtr. 1 through the verse, until the lead (Gtr. 2) enters at measure 5, where it shifts to take that more prominent part. At measure 9, Gtr. 2 drops out, so we jump back to playing Gtr. 1.

Overall, the progression in measures 1–4 is simply "i"—a static C5 power chord. A temporary B♭5 hammers beat 1 of measure 2, but isn't sustained long enough to really impact the harmonic function. Its appearance does, however, foreshadowing the B♭5 chord change at measure 5. Overall, the verse utilizes an eight-measure progression: Cm for four measures, then B♭–F–Cm–Cm. This works out to i, then ♭VII–IV–i. With the bluesy vocal stylings set against big ♭VII–IV-i progressions, the feel seems to recall Whitesnake vividly. The lead at measure 7 acts to answer the vocal "pain" with a straight C minor pentatonic lick.

In measures 9–12, the verse's opening guitar line is developed a bit, adding 4th dyad E♭5 power chords. Rather than acting as any type of progression, these simply function as accents and create an overall Cm7 harmonic quality.

A second lead "answer" comes in the form of slide guitar at measures 15–16. With the slide on your ring finger, pull it up the neck a bit sluggishly. And remember, the target of each note is directly above the metal fret itself, not above the fret spaces where you normally play. To produce vibrato, move your entire hand (including the slide) up and down, centering the motion on the correct pitch. The notes here are drawn from C minor pentatonic, except for the brief upward pull of E♭ to E natural (minor 3rd to major 3rd). This blues move borrows temporarily from the parallel major key, and results in the characteristic blurring of major/minor tonality.

The guitar loosely follows the vocal melody in the pre-chorus (measures 17–24). Here the progression A♭–E♭–B♭–F–Cm works backwards through the cycle of fifths, or "upward." That is to say, each subsequent chord is actually a fifth higher than the one previous to it. Yet, each chord is also a member of the C minor key family. Now let's consider the guitar line. Over A♭, Ritchie plays E♭ (5th) then A♭ (root); over E♭ we see a B♭ (5th). In measure 18, over B♭, the guitar hits D (3rd) then bends to target E♭ (4th) before releasing back to D (3rd). At F, he is still sustaining D, which forms a temporary major-6th suspension that quickly falls to C (5th).

At measure 19, the bend to G anticipates Cm by a half beat. So far, so good: G is simply C's 5th. But things look a little odd as we pick up into measure 20. The Eb-to-C move at beat 4 of measure 19 is derived from the C minor pentatonic box 4 shape. Next, Blackmore shifts to C *major* pentatonic, grabbing D (2nd) and pushing it up a full step to E (major 3rd), sustaining over the bar line, then releasing and completing the lick with a C-A-C (root-6th-root) move.

The melody of measures 21-22 acts as a mirror image to that of measures 17-18. Then we have another bluesy C minor lick. It is played in eighth position, C minor pentatonic box 1, turning to the C blues scale at F# in beat 4.

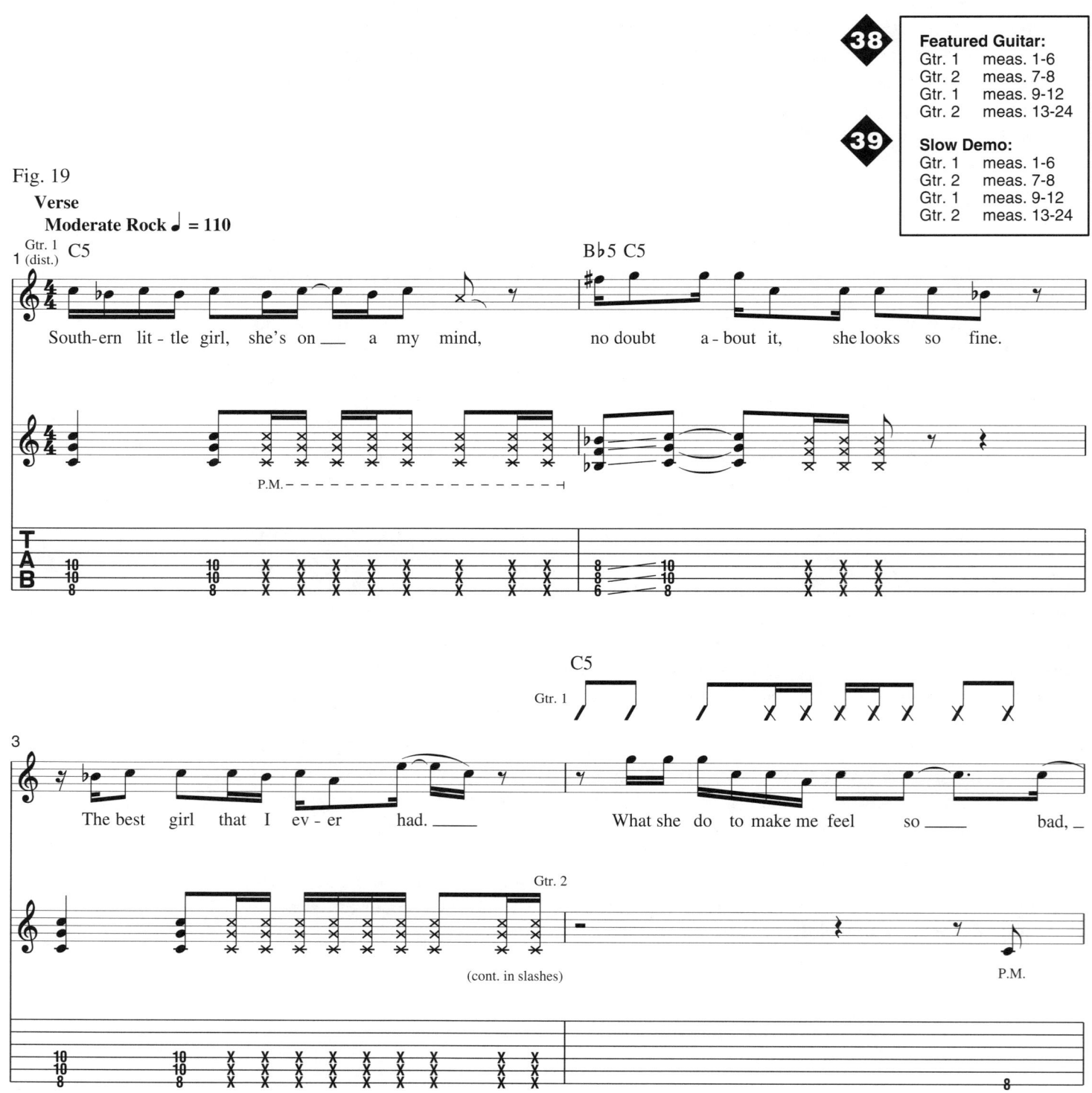

Figure 20–Guitar Solo

Very difficult phrasing and bending techniques combine here to produce a solo that is downright *strange*. And in its oddness lies its undeniable genius. The key is F minor.

Measure 1 opens with a gradually rising 1 1/2 step bend from C at the fifth fret, third string. In terms of fretboard-shape "signposts," we are in F minor pentatonic box 2 here. Holding the peak of the bend, it is then picked with a slight pick harmonic, released, and then vibratoed for a moment before pulling off to B♭ (4th) and hammering again at C (5th).

Next, Blackmore opts for the F minor pentatonic box 3 area, but plays diatonically. First he hits G (2nd) and bends up a minor-3rd interval to B♭ (4th). Then he releases the bend partially, coming down a whole step to A♭ (♭3rd), which itself is still bent up a half step. (If you're looking for fretboard shapes, you won't see any here unless you convert the bent notes to their unbent equivalents—a good idea to be sure.) Next comes another G (2nd) followed by an F–G (root–2nd) hammer-on. Shifting to string 3, we see E♭ (♭7th) and D (6th), suggesting the modality of F Dorian at this point. Descending chromatic tone C♯ leans on and falls quickly to C (5th). This is followed by a quick position shift to F minor pentatonic box 1, although non-pentatonic tones are added soon enough.

Things get really weird with the gradual bending into measure 5. E natural (major 7th) pushes up past the tonic to G (2nd) and glides back down. Then a vibrato bar dip comes up to E♭ (♭7th), now a chromatic half step down. Next, B is bent up a full step to C♯ (♯5th), followed by a dive-bombing open A string, which obliterates pitch considerations altogether! A hammer-on "from nowhere" to high E♭ (♭7th) on string 3 is then lowered and wavered with the bar.

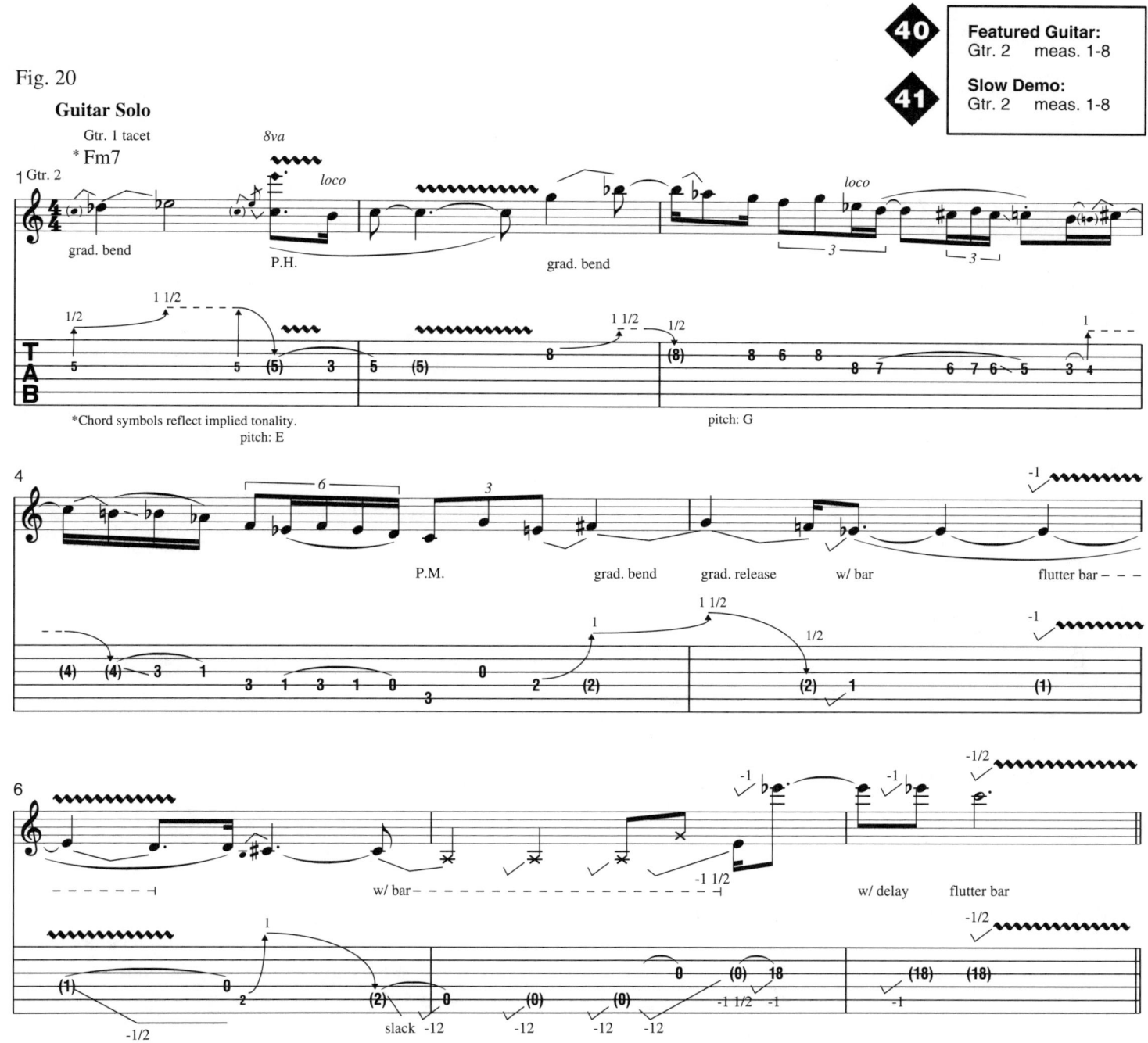

Guitar Notation Legend

Guitar Music can be notated three different ways: on a *musical staff*, in *tablature*, and in *rhythm slashes*.

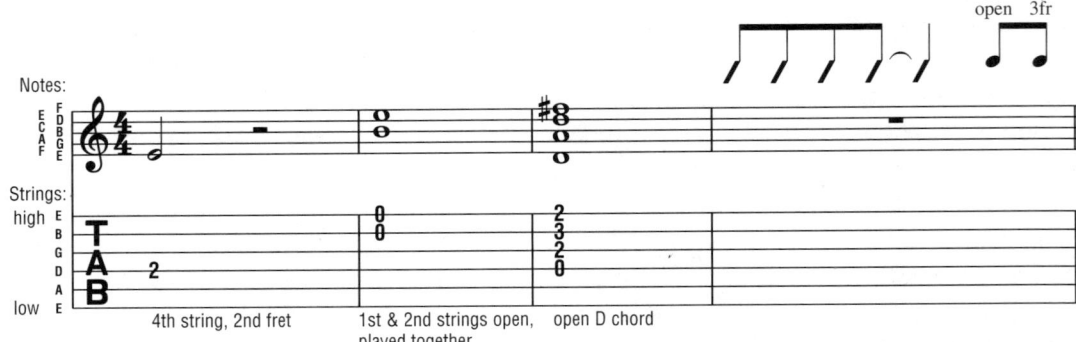

RHYTHM SLASHES are written above the staff. Strum chords in the rhythm indicated. Use the chord diagrams found at the top of the first page of the transcription for the appropriate chord voicings. Round noteheads indicate single notes.

THE MUSICAL STAFF shows pitches and rhythms and is divided by bar lines into measures. Pitches are named after the first seven letters of the alphabet.

TABLATURE graphically represents the guitar fingerboard. Each horizontal line represents a string, and each number represents a fret.

HALF-STEP BEND: Strike the note and bend up 1/2 step.

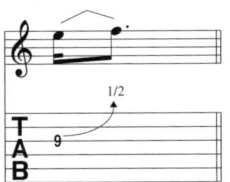

WHOLE-STEP BEND: Strike the note and bend up one step.

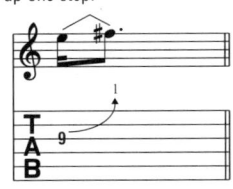

GRACE NOTE BEND: Strike the note and immediately bend up as indicated.

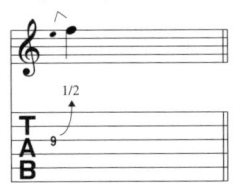

SLIGHT (MICROTONE) BEND: Strike the note and bend up 1/4 step.

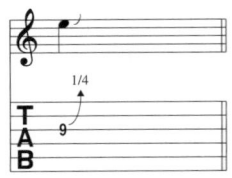

BEND AND RELEASE: Strike the note and bend up as indicated, then release back to the original note. Only the first note is struck.

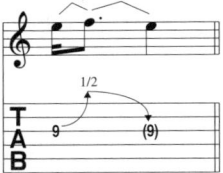

PRE-BEND: Bend the note as indicated, then strike it.

VIBRATO: The string is vibrated by rapidly bending and releasing the note with the fretting hand.

WIDE VIBRATO: The pitch is varied to a greater degree by vibrating with the fretting hand.

HAMMER-ON: Strike the first (lower) note with one finger, then sound the higher note (on the same string) with another finger by fretting it without picking.

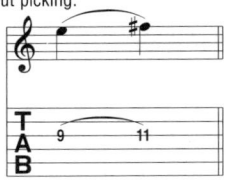

PULL-OFF: Place both fingers on the notes to be sounded. Strike the first note and without picking, pull the finger off to sound the second (lower) note.

LEGATO SLIDE: Strike the first note and then slide the same fret-hand finger up or down to the second note. The second note is not struck.

SHIFT SLIDE: Same as legato slide, except the second note is struck.

TRILL: Very rapidly alternate between the notes indicated by continuously hammering on and pulling off.

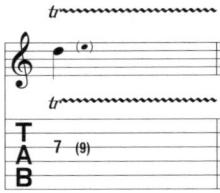

TAPPING: Hammer ("tap") the fret indicated with the pick-hand index or middle finger and pull off to the note fretted by the fret hand.

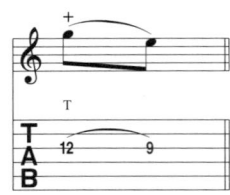

NATURAL HARMONIC: Strike the note while the fret-hand lightly touches the string directly over the fret indicated.

PINCH HARMONIC: The note is fretted normally and a harmonic is produced by adding the edge of the thumb or the tip of the index finger of the pick hand to the normal pick attack.

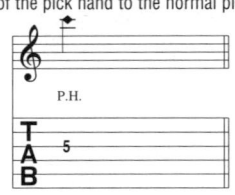

PICK SCRAPE: The edge of the pick is rubbed down (or up) the string, producing a scratchy sound.

MUFFLED STRINGS: A percussive sound is produced by laying the fret hand across the string(s) without depressing, and striking them with the pick hand.

PALM MUTING: The note is partially muted by the pick hand lightly touching the string(s) just before the bridge.

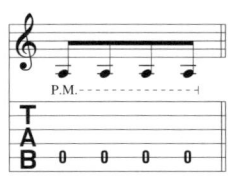

RAKE: Drag the pick across the strings indicated with a single motion.

TREMOLO PICKING: The note is picked as rapidly and continuously as possible.

VIBRATO BAR DIVE AND RETURN: The pitch of the note or chord is dropped a specified number of steps (in rhythm) then returned to the original pitch.

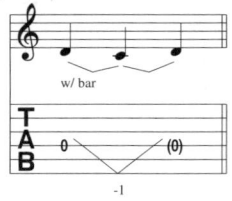

VIBRATO BAR SCOOP: Depress the bar just before striking the note, then quickly release the bar.

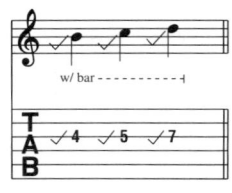

VIBRATO BAR DIP: Strike the note and then immediately drop a specified number of steps, then release back to the original pitch.

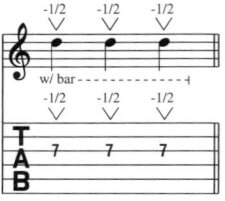